Don't Pee on My Leg
and Tell Me
It's Raining

To Darline,

My mentor and
inspiration in life.

Your Biggest fan,
Judge Judy

Don't Pee on My Leg and Tell Me It's Raining

America's Toughest Family Court Judge Speaks Out

Judy Sheindlin

with Josh Getlin

HarperPerennial
A Division of HarperCollins*Publishers*

The names of the children, other litigants, and family members that appeared in court before me have been changed in order to protect their privacy, with the exception of a few cases that became well-known and were reported in the media or otherwise published. In those cases the names have not been changed.

A hardcover edition of this book was published in 1996 by Harper-Collins Publishers.

HarperCollins books may be purchased for educational, business, or sales promotional use. For information please write: Special Markets Department, HarperCollins Publishers, Inc., 10 East 53rd Street, New York, NY 10022.

First HarperPerennial edition published 1997.

Designed by Alma Hochhauser Orenstein

The Library of Congress has catalogued the hardcover edition as follows:

Sheindlin, Judy
    Don't pee on my leg and tell me it's raining : America's toughest family court judge speaks out / Judy Sheindlin with Josh Getlin. — 1st ed.
      p.   cm.
   ISBN 0-06-017321-1
   1. New York (State). Family Court (City of New York) 2. Juvenile courts—New York (N.Y.) 3. Juvenile justice, Administration of—New York (N.Y.) 4. Juvenile justice, Administration of—United States. I. Getlin, Josh. II. Title.
   KFN5116.5.Z9S54   1996
   346.74701'5'0269—dc20
   [347.4706150269]   95-46424

ISBN 0-06-092794-1 (pbk.)

   99 00 01 ❖/RRD 20 19

For Murry, Ethel, Jerry, and Elaine

Contents

Acknowledgments

My parents gave me spirit, a work ethic and a sense of humor. I grew up with the security of their unqualified love. That security should be the birthright of every child. My husband, Jerry, is the excitement in my life and my friend. I love him so much, I married him twice. His encouragement, support and pride in his often outspoken wife are constants. And our children—Greg, Jamie, Jon, Adam and Nicole—who taught me patience, tolerance, and thrift also provided some great material for the book. Finally to the Hon. Edward I. Koch and the Hon. Allen G. Schwartz, who thought I would be a good judge and gave me the opportunity.

JUDY SHEINDLIN

First and foremost, I want to thank my wife, Heidi Evans, for her love and wisdom. I could not have finished this book without her keen critical eye and endless good humor. My parents, Jules and Ellen Getlin, taught me the importance of values, and they, too, deserve thanks. My mother-in-law, Sara Frantz, contributed her share of insights—along with platters of skirt steak—and her late husband, Raymond, taught me that debunking authority was not only a right, but an obligation.

I also want to thank Pam Forrester and Nancy Blades for their help with child care and parent care. They gave us—and this book—the gift of free time.

Last but not least, two people deserve very special thanks from us both: Diane Reverand, our editor, guided us with a sure hand and keen creative vision. Our agent, Jane Dystel, was the wind at our backs. She believed in this book from the very beginning, and her skill, intelligence and enthusiasm helped turn a great idea into the volume you now hold in your hands.

JOSH GETLIN

Don't Pee on My Leg and Tell Me It's Raining

Introduction
Enough Is Enough

It was just another tragedy in family court.

He was fourteen, 160 pounds, and stood before me pleading guilty to sodomizing his five-year-old cousin. His mother, twenty-nine and clearly zonked on drugs, sat next to him, her head resting on her hands.

The five-year-old cousin and her two brothers had been entrusted by the city to the care of this "lady," who had been qualified as a foster mother. She got control of the children when they were taken from their biological mother, who had abused them.

The teenage boy had been their regular baby-sitter, as his mother was rarely at home. So who was to blame? Everybody, it seems, was a victim.

The boy's lawyer passionately argued for his parole,

since he clearly suffered from his mother's neglect. The crime, he explained, was induced by the stress of being left to care for his three cousins. He was the victim.

Then the boy's mother began to scream that it was all the city's fault, because she had not been given a homemaker to help her care for the children. When I asked why she didn't hire a baby-sitter with some of the $2,000 a month she was getting as a foster mother, the woman answered that she had other expenses. Sure you do, I thought to myself, like feeding your crack habit. She, too, was a victim.

Next, the city attorney argued that the social worker who was supposed to be supervising this foster home had taken extended leave and, owing to dire fiscal constraints, no new social workers had been assigned. Aha! I thought. The city was the victim.

I was beginning to wonder whether I would ever find someone, anyone, willing to acknowledge responsibility for this loathsome situation. Tap-dancing around responsibility has become an art form in my courtroom—and in American society.

As a family court judge, I look down on a daily pageant of dysfunction that would curl your hair. Think of every social problem you can that affects America's disintegrating families—welfare abuse, juvenile violence, abandoned or abused children, ugly custody fights—and you have just begun to scratch the surface of what parades through my court.

After twenty-four years in court, I have come to realize that these are not just legal problems in a downtown building. They are a mirror of what has gone wrong in America, a reflection of how far we have strayed from personal responsibility and old-fashioned discipline. Family courts are a microcosm of social ills, and virtually every one of the forty or so cases I deal with each day convinces me that the time for change was yesterday. The time to wake up is now.

That, in a nutshell, is the message of this book. But before I get into the heart of this, you should know something about me and where I come from. If someone is going to ask you to read 238 pages and tell you what has gone wrong in our society, the least they can do is give you an idea of their background and qualifications.

My career in family court began in 1972, when I was hired by the city to prosecute cases involving juvenile delinquents. Within a month I knew that I had found my professional home. I loved my work and soon developed a reputation as a no-nonsense prosecutor.

Most of the kids during those early years were involved in petty thefts, but as the seventies passed into the eighties, the ferocity of juvenile crime increased. These delinquents were a new breed. And the system did not have a clue how to treat them. We still don't in the nineties, when crimes committed by kids are Xerox copies of those committed by their adult counterparts.

A peek into my private life is important, because it has given me some firsthand perspectives in dealing with the family disputes I must resolve. I was born in 1942 in Brooklyn, New York. My father, Murry, whom I idolized, was a dentist. My mother, Ethel, a remarkable woman, ran my father and the rest of the world. I have a brother, David, five years my junior, who is also a dentist.

I married my first husband when I was twenty and in law school. He was and is a nice guy. My mother liked him and I thought I was ready. Our marriage ended twelve years and two children later, when we no longer shared the same dreams and our home was no longer a happy place for our children. I was already a lawyer working in family court, and was determined that my personal divorce process would be different from the knock-down, drag-out fights I saw every day.

By and large, I was successful, and my former husband remains a friend and, more important, a good father.

I married Jerry Sheindlin when I was thirty-three. It was a love affair from the moment I saw him. He was perfect: handsome, smart, funny, emotionally complex and very needy. I knew that marriage to him would be a lifelong project, and since I always was in need of a project, it was a match.

Jerry's divorce had been less amicable but still relatively civilized. He had three young children; they are all grown now and I love them as if they were my own. Jerry and I always say that together we have five children, and with the addition of three fabulous grandchildren, we have been truly blessed.

In 1982, I was appointed by Mayor Edward I. Koch to the family court bench. Six months later, my husband, Jerry, who had been a defense lawyer for two decades, was appointed to the criminal court bench. We were now a two-judge family, but as the junior jurist, he still took out the garbage.

Jerry and I were both assigned to Bronx court; I in family court, he in criminal court. In 1986 I was appointed the supervising judge in Manhattan and Jerry was elevated to the Supreme Court. In addition to my administrative responsibilities, I preside over trials daily, and since my appointment I have probably heard over twenty thousand cases. Some are just difficult, others are excruciating.

I hear cases involving juvenile delinquents, custody, visitation, child neglect and abuse, paternity, child support, adoption, domestic violence, guardianship and the termination of parental rights. From the beginning, I was committed to becoming proficient—not only in the law, but in the machinations of the various systems that translated the orders I made into practical solutions.

After more than two decades, I have become adept at both. But sadly, I have concluded that the systems barely function, rendering many of my orders empty promises. Part of the problem is that too many people have come to expect too much from government. And the assorted social service systems, however well-intentioned, are crumbling under the sheer numbers of people who look to government first, instead of relying on themselves and focusing on government as a last resort.

Somehow, we have permitted irresponsible behavior to be socially acceptable and have set up an elaborate bureaucracy that encourages lack of individual responsibility, thereby ensuring the longevity of both.

During my years in family court, I have seen a dramatic deterioration in the lives of adults and children. At the same time, there has been a dramatic increase in expensive public programs. We are spending a fortune and the result is failure. The recipients of these monies are in the same or worse shape than before, and the consequences are all around us:

More and meaner delinquents
More unwanted children
More abused children
More dysfunctional adults
More teenage pregnancies

By shifting the emphasis from individual responsibility to government responsibility, we have infantalized an entire population.

There are those who feed from the public trough as recipients; there are service providers who stay up nights, conjuring up in their insomnia ever more wasteful ways to spend our money. There are executives and legislators whose eye on the next election causes gridlock and impotence; there is a judiciary whose vision of reality dates back to Spanky and Our Gang. And there is the media, which transforms villains into victims, manipulates our sensibilities and makes all of us feel guilty.

Our government has spent decades and billions exploring the root causes of crime, violence, teen pregnancy, drug abuse and welfare dependency. We have been exploring forever; now it is time to discover.

That, my friends, is the fundamental point of this book.

By peeling away the layers of dishonesty and hypocrisy that blanket so many social programs, we can discover the underlying problems that face us— and how best to solve them. We need to be truthful and direct, because the time for playing games with people's lives and our precious resources is over.

Don't Pee on My Leg and Tell Me It's Raining is divided into three parts. The first offers an overview of our crumbling system, including the courts, the problems of juvenile delinquency and the weak judicial response to them. The second section zeros in on the huge price we pay for this failure in terms of welfare, foster care and the custody battles that tear apart so many homes. The last section shows the underlying reasons for our failure, including the lack of responsibility and honesty in American society, the scams pervading our national life and, lastly, the myopia of a media that, despite its vast power to do good, is too often asleep at the switch.

People often ask me if there are any bright spots in my workday. Despite the gloom and despair that passes before me, there are indeed some satisfying moments, although they are few and far between. They are the kind of stories that offer a glimmer of hope, and I will discuss them in a concluding chapter, as well as some final thoughts on how we can get out of this mess.

While I don't profess to have all the answers, this book offers solutions that are practical, reality-based and cost-effective. If you read them and agree, tell your friends and my publisher. The pooh-bahs of the politically correct will surely marshal their forces and be out for my head.

Let us send them a message that reads, "Enough is enough."

For me, there is no other choice. I have reached the point in my career where I simply do not care about what is politically correct. Clearly, writing this kind of book forecloses any chance that I might continue my work on the family court bench. By playing it safe, by keeping silent, I would become part of the problem, rather than part of the solution. As a woman, a mother and a judge who has seen our criminal justice system deteriorate for nearly a quarter of a century, I have had it. Writing this book—and sharing my thoughts with you—is worth any inconvenience I might later experience. The price of silence, of ignoring a serious problem, is much too high.

I have given my job 110 percent of my energy for the past twenty-four years. I have been diligent and responsible, and I feel comfortable in saying that there are very few who know the family court system better than I do. However, even with all that energy, the positive results I have seen are few. There is a consistent lack of responsibility among the people I encounter and an institutional chaos that is pervasive. Simply working hard has produced negligible results: doing my job well has not ensured that children are growing up better, that families are thriving or that the city is going to be a better place.

It is hard for me to leave a job that I have tried to do well. But in writing this book, I hope to strip away the veil of secrecy that has protected a social system run by reality-impaired ideologues. It would be an important first step toward some long-overdue change, and a risk worth taking.

CHAPTER 1

Don't Pee on My Leg and Tell Me It's Raining

My father was a very wise man who hated dishonesty more than he hated stupidity. In my second semester of college, I tried to explain why I was getting less than stellar grades and I blamed it on my roommate. She had accidentally gotten pregnant, I told him, and it had distracted me. It was impossible for me to concentrate, I said, when a smile appeared on his face. I was the apple of his eye and he my hero—but he gave me a knowing look and said, "My darling Judy, don't pee on my leg and tell me it's raining."

I think back on my father's words when I start my day as a judge in New York Family Court. Actually, his words haunt me. They should be etched on the courtroom walls. Maybe then the folks lined up outside would get it: I have no time, no room, for excuses and tales of victimization, usually by victimizers. They are all designed to minimize responsibility, individual and bureaucratic.

The price we pay for this buck-passing is staggering.

To show you why, I am going to share some of the stories I have encountered in family court. Instead of snowing you with statistics and mind-boggling studies, these everyday tales tell it all.

Let's begin with an ordinary day in court. The first cases are heard at nine-thirty A.M., and the hallways outside my courtroom are usually packed with people. The cast of characters is extraordinary. They range from juvenile delinquents who make up incredible stories about why they rob and sell crack, to mothers who keep bearing drug-addicted, AIDS-infected babies and indignantly tell the court to butt out of their lives. You'll get a glimpse of middle-class people who cheat the system, rapists who try to cut brazen deals for lesser penalties, indolent fathers who won't support their families and the cold-blooded young killers who have become all too familiar. Our social welfare system is collapsing in this country, so consider this opening chapter a road map to ruin.

After a look at an ordinary day in family court, I think you will agree with me that there are two kinds of people in the world: ulcer givers and ulcer getters.

My mother always said it is better to give than to receive—and she was right.

Kids Deal the Darnedest Things

First up is Elmo, fifteen, who weighs 160 pounds and has an IQ of 90. He has been charged for a second time with selling crack cocaine to an undercover police officer. His lawyer, a young, passionate fellow, argues that Elmo should be released to his mother's custody because he is really a good kid. His troubles started eight months ago, when his grandmother died, the lawyer claims. In his grief, Elmo had no choice but to deal the hard stuff.

"Get a better story!" I fire back, startling the boy, who has a smug look on his face. "Nobody goes out and sells drugs because Grandma died!"

Next is Tito, a delinquent who confesses to mugging an eighty-year-old man in broad daylight. He had to do it, Tito says, because his older brother had just been sent upstate for murder. He was very close to his brother, the boy's lawyer insists, and his crime was a result of post-traumatic stress.

"You'll have to do better than that," I snap. "Some poor man has a cracked skull, and all you're doing is feeling sorry for yourself!"

Then comes a woman, we'll call her Joyce, who is addicted to crack. She already has two crack-addicted babies to her credit, and she didn't report to her drug rehab program as she had promised. Her excuse: She lost the address.

"What do you want, a road map?" I exclaim. "Get real!" I guarantee, she could find a crack den in Albania.

Minutes later, I am looking at the well-dressed lawyers for an alleged charitable organization who are trying to convince me that it costs forty dollars a day to transport a two-year-old baby to a school for speech therapy that is fourteen blocks from his home. This is in *addition* to the $200 daily cost of the therapy, they explain.

"That's $1,200 per week for a toddler!" I say. "Where do you think all that tax money comes from? The tooth fairy?"

Welcome to my world.

It Is Better for the Child to Cry Once Than for Society to Cry Forever

You deal with these problems the way you would deal with any crisis in a family: by showing compassion and setting strict limits. As the mother of five children, I know you have to get tough at the same time that you show love. Without respect and discipline, you might as well give up the game. Family court should be no different. The exact same psychology applies.

Patience is a virtue for any parent, but I have no patience with arrogant punks who shun responsibility for violent crimes. I have no patience with stoned-out grandmothers, absentee fathers or teenage mothers. I have no patience with militant loudmouths who tell you that criminals are not responsible for what they do, or with politicians who campaign on anticrime platforms, then do little or nothing when safely in office.

I wish I could say the same about many of my colleagues in the family and criminal courts. Many times I drive to work thinking about cases like those I just described and wonder—how many of my fellow judges will fall for this bull today? Unfortunately, too many still treat delinquents in 1995 as misguided children and adult criminals as victims of society's neglect. Their benevolent philosophies have made our courts the joke of the street. Crime is exploding, kids have no limits and the punishments we mete out are laughable.

I think back to my father's words when I hear lawyers or defendants making lame excuses for violent behavior. And I ask you: At what point do we all say enough is enough? It is time to take responsibility for our actions.

Maybe I am expecting too much. If people do not have respect for a system of law, you cannot really believe that they will grow up overnight and start acting like responsible adults. If hustlers think they can scam the system and make a mockery of the process, there is surely no percentage in toeing the line.

Sometimes all I can do is scare the hell out of them.

I send a tough message to first-time offenders every chance I get. Maybe then there will not be a second offense. If I am on my game, a male delinquent will find his time in my court to be the second worst experience of his life—circumcision being the first. When some punk in Reeboks acts up, I give him some attitude he will never forget—the very real threat of a one-way ticket to an upstate detention facility. "I'll send you so far upstate," I like to say, "your mother will need a passport to visit you!"

That usually gets their attention. Often the problems are so overwhelming, the procession of fools, incompetents and rip-off artists so long, I do not know where to start.

Criminals, Not Society, Are Responsible for Crime

I keep reminding myself of one basic philosophical truth: Home, school and communities all have a hand in raising our children. In that order. In this country, we have it backward.

Too many homes are dysfunctional because parents or kids are out of control. Yet we fail to hold anyone responsible. We do not know how. Since America will not ask parents to do their jobs, we turn to the schools. But they are in worse shape than ever. They are getting a steady stream of kids who have few learning skills and almost no sense of civilized behavior.

We expect these schools to teach not only the three R's but also morality and ethical standards—and that amounts to two jobs, neither of which they do well. Finally, we turn to the community. Translation: to the taxpayers. We ask them to pick up the costs of educating, incarcerating, healing and housing these youngsters. That is a complete reversal of what should be going on.

Let us get one thing straight: It is the *home* that is screwing up. We should stop making excuses for mothers and fathers who abdicate their parenting responsibility. The home has created these problems, and parents should be the ones to fix it. But who has the courage to speak out about this in public? These days, people who try to tell the truth are called insensitive, ignorant, shortsighted—or worse.

We Have Expected Nothing, and Have Gotten What We Expected

More than 90 percent of the people who come before me receive some kind of handout. Whether it is welfare, social security disability, foster care grants, monthly checks from charitable organizations, the list is endless. And too many of these recipients are ripping off the system. To put it bluntly, they are picking our pockets. They are doing it by the numbers—using the system's own idiotic rules to play a profitable and unconscionable game with our hard-earned tax dollars.

We could have put a stop to this years ago if we had our priorities in order. Everyone knows, for example, that kids need an education to have any hope for the future. If they drop out, they lose hope, and if they are too young or too stupid to equate the two, parents should make sure they get the point. Most of the kids I see come from homes supported by public assistance. It makes sense to insist that children stay in school for them to remain on the welfare rolls.

If a sixteen-year-old decides to drop out of school and joyride through life, all government support to that child should be cut off. The only way public assistance should continue is if the teenager works. And the kind of work is unimportant. Even the most menial and unpleasant labor carries the message that society will not reward deadbeats. Our message should be clear to kids, families and the community: If you want to eat, you have to work. If you stay in school, we will support you. Otherwise, support yourself. No exceptions.

Take Responsibility for Your Life—and Take Your Hands Out of Our Pockets

Does it sound like I am cracking down on the poor? Far from it. Middle-class parents who traipse through my courtroom—blaming everyone from the president to the principal for their children's behavior—fare no better than welfare cheats. Earning a salary should not exempt you as a parent from fundamental responsibilities. If a middle-class kid drops out of school, the $2,000 tax break their parents claim for him should be eliminated. Period. Let us put an extra box on tax returns that requires proof that a child attends school. Without that proof, you lose the exemption. I think you would see a lot more kids back in class if we hit Mom and Dad in the wallet—where it hurts—at tax time.

Nobody dares come up with these solutions. Instead, we have sanctioned a near total breakdown of responsibility. We have infantilized not only teenagers, but adults, grandparents and whole families. No one, it seems, is responsible for their actions in this country! We are all victims!

It reminds me of the condominium story: A Spanish-speaking man once came before my court. A lawsuit charged that he had fathered a child yet failed to provide financial support. He denied that he was the father, and I explained that he certainly had a right to trial. But recent blood tests strongly suggested that he was, in fact, the biological dad. He looked at me in disbelief and said angrily: "Judge, that couldn't possibly be my kid!" Why? I asked. "Because," he answered, "I was wearing a condominium." I told him that his condominium obviously had a hole in the roof.

That one time, science helped us pin the tail on the donkey. But assigning responsibility is not always that easy, especially since we seem to have a national aversion to making people clean up their own messes. Isn't that one of the first lessons we learn in life? Or is America one big kindergarten?

I cannot make it any clearer: A delinquent is responsible for his crime. Men and women are responsible for bearing unwanted, unnurtured children who become society's burden. Parents are responsible for teenage children having children. Legislators are responsible for not addressing the realities of disintegrating families and mushrooming juvenile violence. Bureaucrats are responsible for winking at fraud and flagrant waste of taxpayers' money. Political and racial racketeers are responsible for the breakdown in civilized debate when these issues command attention. The media is responsible for letting knee-jerk compassion get in the way of tough social analysis. And, finally, all of us are responsible for what has happened to American society.

We have to put our collective foot down and demand better. We have tried kindhearted and costly social programs. We have tried blaming ourselves as a community. We have had committees, commissions, blue-ribbon panels and other study groups tinker with social problems at great expense, using all kinds of theories. The bottom line is always the same: spend more money. I have never read a study that concluded that people must take responsibility for their own lives.

When Does What Is Right Take Priority over What Is Politically Correct?

I wrestle with this problem every day. Here is an example:

A young man standing before me is accused of raping an eight-year-old child. It is clear that Tyrone, fourteen, is at least mildly retarded, and in all probability this little girl has not been his only victim. She had been placed in Tyrone's home as a foster child, the fourth one who has been in and out of that home. There is physical evidence indicating the child has been raped, and the city attorney requests that Tyrone be tested for the HIV virus.

That is not an unreasonable request, considering our times and Tyrone's dubious track record. But the law in New York, as in other states, precludes such testing because of some misguided notion of confidentiality. You cannot test criminal defendants for AIDS without their consent, even when they are guilty of rape. In recent years, adult rapists have been using this loophole to plea-bargain themselves down to minimal or no jail time.

The game goes something like this: Tyrone, through his attorney, tells me he will consent to being tested for HIV, thereby letting the victim know whether her life has been further traumatized. But he will do so only if the district attorney lets him off with a plea to a lesser crime, giving him less jail time. Is that all right? I am asked. Of course it's not, and I tell Tyrone and his attorney so. Sounds to me as if the tail is wagging the dog.

Terrible, right? It gets worse. Each week, I see babies born to drug-addicted, HIV-positive mothers. Under present laws, these infants cannot be tested for AIDS without the consent of their parents, because— again—that would violate rules of confidentiality. But I ask you: whose confidentiality? I do not think politicians ever dreamed the laws would be distorted this way, because these rules are meant to protect AIDS victims from discrimination, not to shield them from responsibility for violent crimes or infant abuse.

This is not due process. It is a legal atrocity. The system has a way of grinding up the most defenseless victims, in the most heartless way. We use neat-sounding buzzwords, devoid of common sense, and ignore real suffering.

Do You Have a Constitutional Right to Give AIDS to Your Babies?

Take the case of Lottie. She has four kids, and the last two were born HIV-positive. One of them, now three years old, has spent most of his life in a chronic-care facility because he developed full-blown AIDS. Each year the mother has appeared before me, as the city files a petition to extend her son's stay in that special hospital. On the third anniversary, Lottie comes before me again. She is a twenty-eight-year-old woman who is thin, haggard and looks twice her age. I notice her swelling belly and I am afraid to ask if she has another baby on the way. Instead, I read the reports about her son, Robbie, who spends most of the day in his crib. He is a good kid with a sweet face, nurses say, but they only give him routine care, because of the large number of youngsters on the ward. Nobody plays with him. No one visits.

I look at his mother with anger and ask, "How could you not go there and visit him? He needs affection, he needs your touch. You are his mother. Why don't you give him what he needs?" And she answers: "It's too depressing."

Should this woman be permitted to have more children? How do we as a society respond to her? Counseling did not work. Drug rehab programs did not work. The city even directed her to attend parenting classes. It may take years before she dies of AIDS. Why should she be allowed to take six children into the grave with her, after considerable pain—and all at public expense?

If It's Not One Excuse, It's Another

Lottie did not want to be depressed. But Pepe was afraid of getting his hands dirty. He has six children—three in New York, two in the Dominican Republic and one in Virginia. Today he has come before me after failing to pay child support for his three New York kids, all on welfare. I tell him that if he doesn't pay up, he is looking at six months in jail. No problem, says Pepe, with a smile. He tells me he has a new job with the transit authority, and that he needs another two weeks. Then he will be able to pay child support.

Hope springs eternal and I grant the man a two-week adjournment. When Pepe returns, however, he informs me that he has decided to turn down the transit authority job. He has absolutely no intention, he says, of cleaning toilets in the subway. I look at Pepe and tell him that the bathrooms in the subways have to be cleaned. Who does he think should clean them? Me?

I tell him that I have spent years training myself for my job, and my family depends on me. If all you are able to do is clean toilets to support a family, then that is exactly what you do. But I feel like I am talking to the wall. Traditionally, we let the Pepes of this world off the hook. We ask taxpayers to pay for his kids on welfare, and if past experience is any guide, he will laugh off his experience in court and make six more children.

Criminals Are the Loudest When Insisting on Their Rights

Pepe is an outrage, but when it comes to mocking the system, he is nothing compared to the prisoners who clog our dockets with frivolous and sometimes bizarre litigation.

Here is a perfect example of how our legal system, which initially was responding to the problem of brutal prison conditions, permitted felons to abuse the judicial process. Their abuse of the process diminishes the ability of the courts to respond promptly to legitimate cases. In addition to the diminution of court time for real cases, thousands of lawyers and support staff are paid by taxpayers to ensure that every prisoner's gripe gets a judicial airing. I could not care less if a criminal feels deprived because he or she cannot wear their favorite jewelry or believes that their First Amendment right to freedom of speech is infringed on by a rule that precludes them from displaying their gang insignia.

In family court, we are swamped with cases from inmates seeking more visitation rights with children. Others want to be declared the legal fathers of kids they would not blink at if they were on the outside. Now, with plenty of time on their hands, there is no end to the mischief they can cause. They have access to research materials and computers, all at public expense, and judges must respond to their flood of complaints or face censure from a higher court.

Some of the cases leave you gasping for air. Consider the feelings of a grandmother who is caring for two grandchildren after their mother—her daughter—is killed in a rage by her paramour. Suddenly,

Mr. Wonderful wants her to make an eight-hour bus trip and bring his children to visit him in prison. It is a "family visit" to which he is entitled, and once he has learned how to file a lawsuit, he will not give you a minute's peace. One grandmother who faced this very situation told me she would rather join her daughter, wherever she was, than travel with her kids to visit that monster behind bars.

That is how our legal system gets hijacked. Decent, hard-working citizens usually wait years to get a legal claim heard, but these miscreants in jail insist on service *now,* and nothing is too unimportant for them. They want chunky rather than smooth peanut butter. They demand small animals to sacrifice in order to practice their religion behind bars. I believe very strongly that if we cannot get these folks to stop filing clunker lawsuits, at least we can get them to foot the bill. Perhaps we could demand a filing fee. Or maybe we could drop all pretense and say that once you have been incarcerated, you have lost your right to generate frivolous lawsuits.

I May Be Beautiful, Kid, but I'm Not Stupid

It is amazing how far some criminals think they can twist the truth. Take the case of Novick, a blond, blue-eyed kid of fifteen who comes into my courtroom charged with burglary. He lives in a small enclave in the Bronx with his family, where many Albanian nationals have settled. This was his twelfth arrest and yet, according to his record, he has never spent a day in detention! Quite frankly, I cannot understand why. After he is convicted in a trial before me, I send him to a state institution for the maximum period, which is eighteen months. Novick will spend many moons in that facility, and I think he has finally learned a lesson. But the intrigue is just beginning.

One evening about two years later, my husband, by now a Supreme Court judge in the Bronx, told me about this kid Novick, who looks like a choirboy but was just convicted of attempted murder. At a conference, the kid's lawyer was lamenting that his client believed there was a judicial conspiracy against him, since the last judge who sentenced him was also named Sheindlin. The kid claimed all his records were wrong and that he was only fourteen.

He had mastered the art of judicial manipulation, because if my husband believed this fairy tale, Novick's case would be referred to family court with a maximum sentence of eighteen months, instead of eight and one-third to twenty-five years. I told my husband this kid was yanking his chain, and that if he was fourteen today, according to some bogus document, then his first arrest occured when he was six!

In time, Novick produced just such a document. It was a birth certificate from Albania—no doubt procured for two or three good bottles of rotgut, a Hershey bar and a pair of Levi's—attesting that he was only fourteen when the major crime in question was committed. He almost got away with the scam.

I tell this story to illustrate yet another breakdown in our criminal justice process: the resistance by some misguided folks to fingerprinting and photographing juvenile delinquents. If Judge Jerry Sheindlin had not been married to Judge Judy Sheindlin, a gross miscarriage of justice might have taken place. No judge wants to make decisions based on poor information, and if courts cannot rely on accurate data about criminal defendants, we will all pay the price.

There is an easy solution. A juvenile's criminal record should be treated no differently from an adult's. That means fingerprinting, photographing and sharing records between adult and juvenile courts. If a youngster turns his life around, those records can easily be sealed or expunged at age twenty-five. If he or she does not, their record should follow them to the grave. It is unacceptable for citizens to be victimized by these creeps—whether they are fourteen or forty.

Look at it this way: We fingerprint honest people at work for security reasons. Why all the resistance to identifying people who break the law? I have been fingerprinted at least six times. All judges are fingerprinted, as are most civil servants. Why should convicted felons be treated any differently, whatever their age? Some of our most vicious crimes are committed by youngsters these days, and if the tragic case of Maribel Feliciano does not anger you about the near-total breakdown in our criminal justice system, nothing will.

If Your Killer Is Only Fifteen, Are You Any Less Dead?

Maribel Feliciano was a girl of fifteen who was murdered one day on the subway for a pair of earrings. Maribel was on her way home from school with a friend when a group of four girls who had spent the day marauding and robbing strangers ran into her subway car. One of them spotted her large hoop earrings, and the frightened victim was immediately surrounded by these bullies. One of them grabbed her long hair, pulling her face down to her chest, while another stabbed Maribel in the back. She died in the subway car while the four girls fled without their booty. It was just another story on the evening news.

Incredible as it sounds, a quirk in the law permitted three of these girls to escape criminal prosecution. In New York, they could not be tried as adults for murder because they did not actually take the earrings, they only attempted to steal them. Had they been successful, these fourteen- and fifteen-year-olds—those who did not actually wield the knife—could have faced more serious charges. But since they were under sixteen, they could not be charged for felony murder. It was devastating for Mr. Feliciano, as he heard witnesses describe the vicious attack on the honor student and daughter whom he so dearly loved.

There was no question these girls had been accomplices, and I convicted them. At sentencing, their lawyers argued for leniency. After all, they had not actually done the stabbing. Yet I was not moved, because these girls were what I call enablers. But for their actions, Maribel Felicano would be alive today. I cannot tell you how angry I get when lawyers say, "Judge, my client is just a follower. Peer-group pressure made him do it!" I have a message for these attorneys. I will step down from the bench the first day I have a defendant who comes before me and says: "I'm a leader! I take responsibility for my actions! It was me all along!" There have to be some leaders out there. Maybe they are all just avoiding my courtroom.

Juvenile Justice Is Like a Trolley Car— Quaint and Outdated

For Maribel Feliciano's family—and for other victims—juvenile crime is no joke. We have to revise the way we punish young offenders in this country. We are not dealing with kids from the sixties and seventies who stole hubcaps or covered walls with graffiti. Today's punks are robbing, maiming, raping and assaulting with impunity, and our juvenile justice system is rooted in the 1950s. My personal belief is that we have to get kids' attention, and fast. We have to make them fear the courts and what we are capable of doing to them. If we do not, their antisocial behavior will become ingrained, and we will be dealing with a permanent class of criminals.

There are many ways to get kids' attention. A period of detention in a chilly upstate facility can be a great attitude adjuster. Letting a kid know what it is like to be put in handcuffs and sleep in a jail-like setting for two or three days is worth all the anticrime rhetoric on C-SPAN. But it can also create bizarre results. I am reminded of a story from my early years in Bronx Family Court, when a young man who had just spent ten days in detention on his first conviction was brought back before me. Lionel had a lot less swagger now than when he first appeared in my court. He stood there with his brown eyes riveted on me, and I proceeded to throw the book at him.

I call it The Speech, and it goes something like this:

"Lionel," I asked, "did you enjoy your last ten days?" "No," he mumbled. I continued: "I want you to know that I didn't think about you *once* over the last ten days. I went to the movies. I saw my family, and I'd bet even your poor mother was probably relieved not to have to worry about where you were and who you were hanging around with. She got a good night's sleep. And I tell you this, Lionel, because now I'm going to give you some rules for your parole. You break those rules, and I'll send you right back there."

I was in great form, just starting to roll. "You have a seven P.M. curfew," I said. "You're to be in school every day and on time. You're not to associate with any of the people you were arrested with. Do you understand?"

As I spoke, Lionel's eyes became wider and wider. I thought, this is one boy I'm really getting through to! I savored the drama, throwing my robes over my shoulder, tossing my head back, leaning down and staring this kid into the ground. As his eyes grew large, my chest expanded. I had given this spiel before, and soon I reached the point where I asked Lionel which door he wanted to go out—the door at the front of the courtroom, representing freedom, or the door leading back to jail. Suddenly, an aide gave me a handwritten note that read: "Judge, all the buttons on your blouse are open." I looked down and realized that Lionel had been staring not at my face—but at my chest! And when I asked how he wanted to leave the courtroom, he looked at me and answered with a big smile, "Oh, Judge, I want to go home with you!"

CHAPTER 2

This Isn't Kiddy Court; It's Criminal College

When my son Adam was six years old, we lived in a typical suburban home. I was an attorney practicing in Manhattan Family Court. Adam was a beautiful but very precocious child, always looking for an angle or advantage. I used to think that when he grew up, I would be visiting him either at his palatial estate or once a month in some prison upstate.

After a long day of prosecuting delinquents, I pulled into my driveway to find Adam sitting with a box of caps and banging them with a rock to make them explode. Under my rigorous and relentless cross-examination, he finally confessed that he had ridden his bike to the corner store and stolen the caps. This was the test of my parenting; this could be his turning point.

I quickly put Adam in the car and drove to the store, where he sheepishly apologized for the theft. I told the storekeeper that if he ever saw him in the store alone again, to call the police and arrest him. Today, Adam is an assistant district attorney in New York and that story seems very, very old.

Or is it?

They Laugh at the System

When I first confronted Adam with what he had done, he treated it as a game. Just like thousands of other kids who parade through our criminal justice system today. Juvenile violence is skyrocketing across the nation and adults are largely to blame. I cannot tell you how many times I have seen delinquents walk out of our courtrooms, laughing at victims and at the non-punishments they receive. Laughing at the judge and laughing at the system.

The numbers are not funny: In 1979, there were an estimated 70,000 kids in juvenile institutions nationwide. In 1991, the last year for which we have such figures available, the number rose to more than 90,000. In 1994, the Criminal Justice Institute estimated that 100,000 or more kids were in custody, in adult as well as juvenile facilities. In cities, suburbs and rural communities we see the same stories on television every night about youngsters breaking the law and winding up behind bars. We hear the same heart-wrenching stories from victims, the same cries of parents, educators and law enforcement officials: Where have we gone wrong, and how can we fix it?

Let's start with common sense. By failing to set strict limits for children—in the home, in the school and in society as a whole—we aggravate the very problems we're trying to solve. By winking at abuse, covering up criminal behavior or explaining it away, we have created a monstrous dilemma for law enforcement.

In the stories that follow, you will meet delinquents who maim and destroy people just for sport. You will encounter kids who think they can make "deals" and simply walk out of court after committing horrible, senseless crimes. Their excuses are endless, and so are the social shockwaves set in motion by their actions.

Is there an answer? The eight-point program I offer at the end of this chapter is a good place to begin. Some of the suggestions might seem harsh and outrageous, but they're nothing compared to the nightmare of juvenile delinquency and society's impotence in dealing with crime.

Her Life Was Over—for Their Sport

For years, mainly as a prosecutor in family court, I thought of my job as a legal game. There was a winning side and a losing side. You had to play the angles just right. But the case of Stella Schaefer-Epstein changed me forever.

Stella was a doctor who, well into her seventies, still enjoyed a full life practicing her profession. She regularly took walks through New York's Central Park between her office and her home. One summer day the police had been watching a group of teenage girls marauding through the park, clearly up to no good. They were hassling parkgoers and being generally disruptive. Believing that something far worse would happen, the cops kept them under surveillance. And then Dr. Schaefer-Epstein crossed their path. As police watched from the bushes, these girls surrounded Dr. Epstein, knocked her to the ground and grabbed her pocketbook. They were quickly apprehended and whisked away, but Dr. Epstein could not lift herself off the ground and emergency medical services were called. The girls had broken both of her hips.

By chance, I was assigned to prosecute this case. But in order to interview Dr. Epstein I had to wait until she was released from the hospital and resettled in a rehabilitation center in Westchester. I wanted to make certain that I had the story through her eyes, and that she would be willing to testify in court. When I entered her room, this lovely-looking lady was seated in a wheelchair. We spoke for about an hour and she told me about the horrors of that day. She also told me that she was unwilling and physically unable to participate in the court trial. Her life, she said, was over.

For cruel and malicious sport, these girls had destroyed a woman's otherwise full and productive life. Yet my rage toward these delinquents was equaled by my fury at the police. Instead of rounding up these miscreants before they had a chance to wreak havoc, they had waited in the bushes to make sure they had a good collar. It all seemed so senseless. So futile.

Because the police were eyewitnesses, at least I won convictions against all of the girls. But not before their lawyers tried to pull a fast one. The attorney for one fourteen-year-old girl said his client should not be jailed because she was four months pregnant at the time of the attack! The judge, a political hack and a mental midget, bought this sob story and placed her on probation. Meanwhile, the other lawyers argued that if the pregnant girl got a break, their clients also deserved leniency, since they had proved themselves "responsible" by not getting pregnant.

I asked myself—am I the only sane person in this asylum? Years later, I ask myself the same question. Juvenile delinquency is not a game. For the delinquents who enter the system, it should be an excruciating experience that they will never want to repeat.

Preserve the Peace First—Worry About Root Causes Later

The primary obligation of any civilized society must be to preserve the peace and to protect its citizens.

You worry about the lawbreakers and their rehabilitation second. Law-abiding adults, children eager to learn and seniors all have the right to pursue their lives free from fear. But we have lost sight of that in our criminal justice system.

For decades we have put the system under a microscope. Politicians, sociologists, psychologists and social workers have scrambled to find the magic key that will reduce criminal violence in America. Millions have been spent on these efforts, and still we are losing the streets. We are suffering with a third-rate school system. We are forsaking the pleasures of our parks because of teenage hoodlums. And yet, like Don Quixote, we are still tilting against windmills—still looking for the root cause, for the instant cure.

America has to shift directions, and fast. Our first goal must be to ensure public safety. We must stop pandering to racial racketeers who have no real constituency, yet dominate the media and what passes for the discussion of social problems in this country. The vast majority of people—black, white, Asian and the rest—want a quiet, secure community, a place where they can nurture their families. But that will not happen until decent folks take back control of their government.

Let me give you just one example of how misguided and unresponsive legislators unwittingly promote more violence. A fifteen-year-old kid, I'll call him Joe, was arrested twice, once for drug sales and once for robbery. He was found guilty in family court and put in a state institution for the maximum time allowed, eighteen months. The state institution released him after seven months, which was their perogative under existing law. Now sixteen, Joe returned to the street where he was soon arrested again for robbery. At that age, he was considered an adult. But when he went before a criminal court judge, his family court record was not available to the judge. He was treated as a novice in the legal system and released on his own recognizance because, as far as the court was concerned, he had no criminal history.

The story gets crazier: Why, you might wonder, was Joe released after only seven months from the juvenile institution when we sent him away for eighteen months? The answer, according to the facility, is that they did not have enough beds for these kids. Currently in New York, it costs taxpayers $75,000 to incarcerate one delinquent for a year. In some states, the cost is even higher. Somebody is asleep at the switch when we are spending that kind of money and getting such pitiful results. Today, there is a 75 percent recidivism rate among young offenders like Joe when they return to the streets. Can you imagine if you were in business and 75 percent of your products were returned for being defective? You would be out of business in a week. But bureaucrats build careers with such a track record. We taxpayers are paying for a

Rolls-Royce juvenile system and we're getting an Edsel. More expensive, clearly, is not better.

Expediency Breeds Contempt

It certainly does not buy you respect. If I have learned one thing from our criminal justice system, it is that expediency breeds contempt. Especially among kids who think they can get away with murder every time they appear in court. I cannot speak for many of my colleagues, but I do not make deals with fourteen-year-olds. Lawyers are always asking me if I will cut some slack for their clients. If they plead guilty, will I parole them? Will I place them on probation? Will I accept a plea to a misdemeanor in exchange for their cooperation with a special youth program? My standard answer to all such offers: "This is not *Let's Make a Deal*, and I'm not Monty Hall!"

Kids may be used to getting over on the system, but they do not get over on me. I explain that I will be paid the same salary whether I take their guilty plea or try their case. Someone's case is going to be tried in my courtroom today, and it might as well be theirs. I don't deal with delinquents. And of course, that is how you deal with troublesome kids, whether they are yours or somebody else's. You draw the line and get their attention.

It is also true for parents. In November of 1994, a young man appeared before me charged with riding in a stolen car. Not exactly the most serious charge I see, and on the advice of his attorney the young man pleaded guilty to unauthorized use of a motor vehicle, a misdemeanor. The probation department advised me, however, that he had previously pleaded guilty to armed robbery and had been arrested in October for selling drugs.

His lawyer, sensing I was about to put his client in custody, told me that in the previous three weeks, the young man had been doing "beautifully." He had been going to school regularly and seeing his probation officer every Monday. I told the lawyer it was not Mondays I was worried about, and jailed him. Suddenly, the kid's mother went nuts. She screamed that "this is why people spray places like this with machine guns!" She shouted that her boy was a good boy and she would not calm down. This lady had gone too far. I held her in contempt of court and put her in jail.

The lawyers were amazed; they had never seen a judge incarcerate the mother of a juvenile! But I told them I had no choice. If she had no respect for the system—and that had obviously filtered down to her child—then the sight of his mother in handcuffs would be stronger than any lecture I might give him. This lady took no responsibility for her actions, and her son had learned the lesson well. Look what happened to Joe: He committed armed robbery and was rewarded with probation. For joyriding, he thought, he would no doubt get a testimonial dinner! After four hours in one of our malodorous cells, the boy's mother had a change of heart and decided to apologize to me. I let her go—Joe remained in jail.

I Don't Make Deals with Delinquents

Making deals with delinquents only reinforces their antisocial behavior, and the system can be its own worst enemy. Toby, fourteen, liked to rob elderly people and finally got caught. Three of his victims positively identified him, but since there is no such thing as consecutive sentencing in family court—allowing us to extend his punishment based on the number of crimes he has committed—we essentially gave him two freebies. Toby served one sentence for the price of three robberies! Quite a deal. I am sure he was delighted.

But not as thrilled as the young thug whom I sent upstate in November 1993. Three months later, he stood before me on another arrest for robbery. Why, I asked the representative of the state institution, was this boy found in Times Square when he was supposed to be in custody? She looked uncomfortable and shifted from foot to foot, causing me to shout: "This is not Twenty Questions! I want an answer!" Finally, the bureaucrat explained that the boy had been on a "cultural outing" and had simply walked away from his bus. This is some America, folks. You send a kid to jail, and the jailer takes him to the theater.

I wish this was an isolated story, but it is not. In my court, and in courts across America, we get reminders every day that parents are not parenting, schools are not schooling and the social order is just distintegrating. The parade of adolescent criminals is never-ending. They are strong, they are quick and they have no remorse over increasingly ferocious crimes. Understanding their tangled pathology and broken homes can never excuse what they have done. But at the same time, it is just not possible to incarcerate every kid who comes through the courts. Sometimes, you can only shake them up and hope some sense gets through. I try to leave them with the image of a not-so-kindly and rather frightening lady who is on to their tricks.

I do not know how many times kids have told me they "found" the guns they were caught with, and I just will not allow it. Halting the proceedings, I ask the courtroom: "How many people here ever found a gun?" When nobody raises their hand, I turn back to the kid with a stone poker face. "I may be beautiful, but I'm not stupid," I say. "Don't push your luck with me."

The kid's attorney will protest, of course, but I am used to that. Most of the young defense lawyers I see are committed to more than their professional craft. They are committed to a cause. They insist that society has created their clients, and tell me every day that deprivation is an excuse for outrageous conduct. Many of them not only say it, they deeply believe it.

So it was refreshing once to hear a lawyer explain the facts of life to his young client, who had been arrested for selling drugs to an undercover cop. The attorney stood up and said the kid was prepared to plead guilty to criminal possession of a controlled substance. At this, the kid looked astounded, and said: "I didn't tell you I was going to plead guilty! Listen, man, I'm not pleading guilty!" Whereupon his lawyer looked at him and said, "Listen, pal, I don't tell you how to sell drugs. Don't tell me how to practice law!"

My Girlfriend Made Me Do It, and Other Excuses

I wish the lawyer whose client came next had a similar sense of humor. His kid had mugged a tourist from Germany and was caught red-handed by the police, holding both the victim's wallet and his own kitchen knife. The attorney passionately argued that his client should be paroled. He needed the money, not for himself, but for his girlfriend to have an abortion. How noble! I guess he thought I would be moved by this young man's altruism. He was wrong.

Knives, by the way, bring out the worst in some delinquents. During the very next trial, a woman in her forties testified that the young man sitting before me had tried to rob her with a twelve-inch knife. The kid, his name carved neatly in his hair, kept interrupting. His lawyer told him to be quiet, but to no avail.

Finally, the boy jumped to his feet and appealed to me. "Judge!" he shouted, "She's lying! It wasn't a twelve-inch knife! It was a six-inch knife!" Did he think I would cut his sentence in half? He was wrong.

Sometimes you want to grab hold of these kids and just heave them out the door. Like the teenager from Newark, New Jersey, who was caught in the New York Port Authority Bus Terminal with eight ounces of crack cocaine. He and his mother sat in my court while I learned from our probation department that he had been arrested twice in his hometown for drug possession, and had been placed on probation both times. The prosecuting attorney asked me to jail this kid in New York, but that idea offended me. I explained that we had our own criminals in my state, and I was not willing to cough up another $75,000 in tax dollars to rehabilitate a New Jersey resident. I told this drug dealer that we had our own garbage to collect, and unless he was on his way to a permanent address in a New York cemetery it would be unwise for him to set foot in our city again. He might get caught, after all, and could wind up before another judge. Someone who lacked my kindness and compassion.

Did he get the messsage? It was hard to tell. But there was no mistaking the look of astonishment on the face of the fourteen-year-old girl who had the bad luck to wind up in my court after she rearranged the face of a thirty-nine-year-old Indian woman with her Walkman radio. Sometimes girls can be more vicious than their male counterparts, and this young delinquent seemed particularly rough.

She Didn't Say Excuse Me— So I Broke Her Nose

It happened at a subway station on Manhattan's Upper West Side, where the Indian woman and her twelve-year-old son were trying to leave a packed train at rush hour. The car was crowded, and this young girl and her friend were blocking the door. When the woman tried to pass, the teenage girl stood in the doorway and began cursing her. Offended at the use of such language, the victim gave her a dirty look. Whereupon the girl, feeling "dissed," followed the woman off the train and punched her in the face with her Walkman radio, realigning the bridge of the lady's nose. Police quickly arrested the girl.

"She didn't say excuse me when she walked past me," was the girl's only explanation. Then it was my turn. This was the teenager's first arrest, but she had committed an act of violence against another person. She had a history of school truancy and a lousy attitude in my courtroom. The girl probably thought she would get a slap on the wrist, but I had a different message, and put her in detention for ten days. The look of amazement—and fear—on her face was worth it all. There is nothing in our family court sentencing provisions under the category of attitude adjustment. But there should be.

How else do you deal with kids who inflict terror and feel no guilt? I once tried the case of a thirteen-year-old who was target shooting out of his housing project window and killed a sixty-four-year-old woman returning from church. I asked if he had anything to say to the woman's family, who filled my courtroom. But his eyes were blank. He never moved. He had nothing to say.

Foreigners—the Newest Victims

Maybe we should give classes in remorse, along with reading, writing and arithmetic. It might help those kids who have begun to pick on ethnic targets in New York. In recent years, growing numbers of black and Hispanic kids have taken the subway to Chinatown and make no bones about their intentions. They later tell probation officers that they have targeted Asian victims for robbery because many of them are here illegally and are afraid to testify in court proceedings. They make the perfect prey.

Many of these young thugs undoubtedly feel that they are victims. Most come from poor homes and attend second-rate schools with little hope for a happy future. But that is no excuse for criminal behavior, and it is surely no excuse for committing a crime based on the race of the victim. That, my friends, is a bias crime, pure and simple.

Last year, two of these kids picked on an elderly Asian man in a subway station. One teenager put him in a choke hold while the other punched him in the stomach. They rifled through the contents of his suit coat and then let him escape. The old man fled up the stairs of the subway, never to be seen again. But two plainclothes officers watched the crime and made a quick arrest.

When the matter came before me, one defense attorney insisted that I could not possibly convict either boy without testimony by the victim. If he did not appear, the lawyer said, they could never prove that these thugs beat up the old man without his permission and took his money. "You won't get away with that in my country," I answered, "and certainly not in my courtroom." I proceeded with a full trial, taking the testimony of each officer. The defense attorney, no genius and clearly unprepared, asked the fatal question: "How do you know that the money my client had on him didn't belong to him?" he asked one cop. "Because it was yen," answered the officer.

Then there was the thirteen-year-old kid and his fifteen-year-old pal who decided to rob a Chinese takeout store. They cooked up the following plan: The thirteen-year-old, who had supplied the gun, went into the restaurant to ask for change for a $10 bill. "Do you want two fives or singles?" asked the owner. The kid did not care, because it was his job to make sure the owner was alone. He went outside and told his buddy that the store was empty. The fifteen-year-old went back in, aimed the gun at the owner and demanded all his money. When the man did not move fast enough, the boy shot him in the head. He was twenty-nine, hardworking and dead for nothing.

The fifteen-year-old shooter was tried as an adult in Supreme Court, but owing to a quirk in the law, the thirteen-year-old came to my court. No money had been taken and the younger one had not technically used the gun. His lawyer argued for leniency, citing his age and the fact that the murder was committed by another. I wish I could have put him away for twenty years, but all I could do was send him to an upstate facility for three years. So much for justice.

Foreigners—the Newest Criminals

Juvenile delinquency is an equal opportunity crime, and often the shoe is on the other foot. Asian gangs, for example, are among the most vicious in our society. They rob, murder and extort money from their own community. They are as dangerous as they come. These cases are hard to crack because of the fear that gangs engender in the rest of the Asian community. It is hard to get people to testify about them.

Once, when one of these thugs was convicted of

extortion in my court, his father begged me for mercy. He was a kind, hardworking man, and asked that I allow him to send the boy back to his home province in China. There, he would learn the wisdom of a law-abiding life and reform his ways. The young man had already been in detention for two months and I figured this was one way to save the taxpayers $200,000 or more in long-term detention costs. As long as he is back in China, I reasoned, he could not hurt anybody in New York.

Some four months later, however, the court received a letter from this young man begging to be allowed to come back to New York. It turns out that his home province was not what his father had described to him. Just a bunch of dirt farmers, the boy wrote, and he had been picked on because his skin was lighter than other Chinese. His father insisted on bringing him back, and I did not have the power to stop him. But I had the boy detained at Kennedy Airport and brought to my court. I sentenced him to a state institution, and he was on his way within minutes. I could not help but wonder, though, if he thought the residents of his new home were all light-skinned Chinese.

Justice is easy in these cases. But sometimes you stare into the heart of a crisis that defies any rational solution. These are the cases that give you nightmares—no matter how tough or hardened you have grown over the years.

Could Any Punishment Fit This Crime?

One incident in particular stands out. An emergency services team was called to an apartment on Manhattan's Upper West Side, where they were met by a young man who said his sister was violently ill, sitting on the toilet in their home. They found the girl's mother and aunt sitting nervously in the living room. The team entered the bathroom and carefully removed this young girl, who spoke only Spanish, from the toilet seat. At first they saw nothing unusual, but then one officer noticed that the bowl had been covered with toilet paper to hide the surface. When he removed the paper, he found an eight-pound baby boy, headfirst in the water, and already dead.

The girl was arrested for murder, and the case was investigated by the district attorney for a year. Yet they could not decide who was responsible. Consider their dilemma: Two adults were sitting no more than fifteen feet away, and there was no blood in the bathroom. Who had cleaned it? Not knowing what to do, the authorities declined to prosecute and turned the matter over to family court. There, prosecutors charged the girl with second-degree murder. She was thirteen when she had the baby and fifteen when she finally reached my court.

I learned during the ensuing trial that the family were practitioners of Santeria, and had been surprised to learn that the girl was pregnant. By the time this tangled story got to me, there was no easy way to unravel it. Who had delivered the baby? This pretty young girl did not appear to have an IQ above 90. Who had placed the child in the toilet? Clearly, someone was trying to conceal the infant, and the prosecutor insisted on nothing less than a murder conviction, with maximum jail time.

I am nobody's fool, and it does not take much for me to throw the book at criminals. But I asked myself, Jail for whom? For the aunt? For the girl? For the boy who had impregnated her? If I was not mistaken, the girl was now pregnant with yet another child. What were we supposed to do with this heavenly little bundle? Sometimes there are no solutions, only questions. I put the young mother on probation, so we would at least have some supervision over her life. In this case, it seemed, everyone had suffered.

For Some Kids, There's No Redemption

I remember being filled with uncertainty—for all of ten seconds. The very next case jerked me back into the real world. Two young boys had visited a baseball card store and, because they were acting up, the owner threw them out. No doubt they were very angry, and they found the perfect target for their frustration. An elderly Vietnamese woman, well into her eighties, was hobbling down the street with a cane, and for no reason other than sport, one of the boys slapped her in the head with a plastic bag. It was not a very heavy bag, they told me afterward, so when that did not cause sufficient damage, the other boy stuck his leg between hers and tripped her.

She fell to the ground in pain, and the boys were caught by several civilians before they could run away. Police arrested them moments later, charging the teenagers with assault. Yet neither acknowledged any guilt, because they said they had not intended to cause the old woman any harm. They were only fooling around. Just boys being boys. I looked at the bruised arms, legs and face of their eighty-seven-year-old victim and I thought, these kids should be so black and blue. They did not want the woman's money. They did not even know if she *had* any money. It was all done for entertainment.

I remember thinking that I could see into a crystal ball with these punks. Even though they had limited criminal records, the road ahead of them was clear: first juvenile facilities and then prison. For them, there would be no redemption, no rehabilitation. Their sociopathic behavior was fixed.

Our courts are crowded with similar examples of this new strain of ferocity. All we can do is protect ourselves and toughen our laws because we do not know why it happens or how to fix it. We had better do it fast, because the clock is not on our side. Beginning in 1985, we saw a huge number of crack babies entering the foster care system, along with their siblings. Most of us know that foster care programs nationwide have been a disaster, and by 1998, many of these kids will turn thirteen. As the products of dysfunctional homes, too many of them will undoubtedly enter our juvenile justice system. This might be our last chance to do something about their future, and our own safety. Here are a few suggestions:

1. Hard time is good. Good time is a joke.

Convicted juveniles, like adult offenders, often gain early and undeserved release from jail. In my opinion, good time should be earned for productivity; it should not be a reward that accumulates just by stepping inside prison walls. Juveniles should qualify for early release only if they complete a course of academic or vocational studies. Let us reward those who do the right thing, but keep those who are not motivated behind bars for their full term.

Once, when I sat in Bronx Family Court in 1985, I reviewed the case of a fifteen-year-old boy who had three convictions to his credit, two of them violent. I was amazed when the case was called and he was led into court not only in handcuffs, but in leg irons as well. He stood about six foot three and must have weighed 280 pounds. The boy stood there with his mother, his attorney, the prosecutor and a representative of the state institution where he had been confined.

I read the file carefully and learned that this young

man had been in four different facilities, none of which were able to contain his violent behavior. While the state had originally asked that he be confined for an additional twelve months, it had now changed its mind and wanted to release him. Why? I asked. The state's answer was simple and chilling: "We have done all we can for him, Your Honor, and he has exhausted our service," said the representative. I was dumb-struck. He had not only exhausted their services, but clearly had sapped their sanity. Then the young man's mother interrupted, saying, "I don't know what you're going to do with him if you let him go. But he ain't coming home with me!" I did what I believed was the only sane thing, and put him back in custody for another year. Maybe they could not help him, but at least we would know where he was. The idea that he would be out roaming the streets was unthinkable.

2. Reward the productive, not the unproductive.

Taxpayers made it clear in the last election that they are no longer willing to support costly programs that have a long history of failure. Rehabilitation is a laudable goal, but when you spend millions and do not even come close to reaching that goal, it is time for a new broom. We have a special legacy of failure when it comes to changing the lives of youthful offenders, and still the dollars—and the bodies of vic-tims—pile up.

The fact is, we have been focusing on a small

minority of the kids who come from poor, dysfunctional homes. The vast majority of these children suffer from neglected schools and streets, and yet do not commit crimes. Most kids struggle within these chaotic environments, with little or no support, and yet try to do the right thing. But we have ignored them. For years, our social and fiscal emphasis has been on those few who break the law. We leave the good kids to fend for themselves.

A recent set of photographs in my local newspaper illustrated this crazy inversion of priorities. In one picture was a state-of-the-art gymnasium, with Nautilus equipment and gleaming free weights. It was part of the recreational complex at an upstate detention facility. The other photo was an overcrowded, deteriorating inner city junior high school. The paint peeling off the walls and broken windows were symbols of how little we value our law-abiding children.

What kind of insanity is this? We should scale down our juvenile justice facilities and adult prisons to the bare minimum, offering offenders food, clothing and a bed, plus vocational and academic training. Period. Meanwhile, we should take the money we save from "dressing up" our detention facilities and spend it on the good kids who are struggling just to get by. We should let them know that we are doing this to invest in them and their communities, to show that we appreciate their struggle and want them to succeed. We should offer them part-time or after-school jobs. If society does not acknowledge their importance to our future, many more will fall prey to the mean streets.

3. For kids who have a chance, group homes are the answer.

Sometimes, juveniles need more than a program to change their lives. A loving environment can work wonders. Many kids have to be removed from their communities, not because of the ferocity of their crimes, but because they come from dysfunctional homes. From what I have seen, no interventions will fix these parents—certainly not while their children are still children.

Consider the case of George, a fifteen-year-old boy who appeared in family court on his first offense. It was a nonviolent crime and did not appear to be serious. He accepted full responsibility for what he had done, and when I read the probation report describing his history and home life, my jaw dropped.

He had skipped school far more often than he attended, but the reason was heart-wrenching: His father was an abusive alcoholic who regularly beat his mother in their home. George knew that his father became particularly destructive after a drinking binge and so he stayed home to protect his mother. She was unwilling to file charges, and George had become the family protector. Here was a young man who, through no fault of his own, had been entirely deprived of a

childhood. Now, he faced the prospect of being institutionalized. To keep him at home meant we would
lose any chance to improve his life. He was doomed to
become a dysfunctional, uneducated adult.

What we need for kids like George are small
group homes. He was not a predator; he was a gentle
and basically moral kid. What he required was a
healthy environment. Given the state of our econ-
omy, many houses these days are cheap. If the state
purchased a $250,000 home to shelter four such
kids—who lived there with in-house parents—these
youngsters might have a decent shot. Obviously, we
would screen these caretakers carefully. We would
want them to have an education and parenting skills.
But think of the numbers: In one year, you would pay
for the cost of the house, considering the $75,000 tab
to house an individual kid in a state facility. Even if
you paid an additional $5,000 per year for food,
clothing and incidentals, you would be saving four
lives—and a lot of money.

4. Let us put reality back into the system— starting with language.

The legislatures of each state should send a clear
message that the priority of the juvenile justice system
is protecting the citizenry. They could begin by
improving their English.

In most states, the trial of a delinquency case has
all the safeguards of an adult trial. Yet we muddy up

the proceedings with a legal jibberish that does not say what it means. It is confusing to everyone—to police, judges, juveniles and, most of all, the public. In New York, for example, a juvenile is not accused of a crime. He is accused of "an act which, if committed by an adult, would be a crime." A juvenile is not called a defendant, but a respondent. A prosecutor is not called a prosecutor, but a petitioner. A trial is called a fact-finding hearing. A sentencing is a dispositional hearing. And a conviction is not a conviction; it is a finding. Can we get some reality in here? If some punk bashes your head with a baseball bat, we should not call this an "incident." We should call it what it is—a crime, a felony. Soupy language is stupid and diminishes the justice system.

We should also eliminate the rules of confidentiality affecting juveniles. Legislators fail to protect the public when they make it impossible for judges to know a young offender's full criminal history at the time of sentencing. They only protect a misguided sense of fairness. We have to abandon old arguments that we are stigmatizing youngsters by making their criminal records available for inspection, or by fingerprinting and photographing them. This is old-fashioned pandering, and juvenile crime stopped being old-fashioned years ago. Citizens have a right to know who is living next door. Do they want a teenage babysitter who also happens to be a convicted drug dealer or sex offender? You cannot make responsible judgements without good information, and that is true whether you are a judge or a neighbor.

5. We need a national curfew.

Most lawbreaking by youngsters takes place at a time when these kids should be at home. If they were reasonably supervised by parents, this would not be a problem. But they are not, and since juvenile crime is skyrocketing, we need stronger protections. I recommend imposing a national curfew for kids under eighteen, and believe me, that is not as harsh as it sounds. When I was growing up, my parents set a curfew for me. On school nights it was nine P.M., and on weekends it was midnight. Maybe you had the same experience, or know someone who did. Either way, you learned to live with those rules. If the parents of today's children cannot or will not set similar limits, then society must do it for them, for their protection—and its own.

6. CCC—career criminal control

Judges should have the option of imposing consecutive sentences on particularly violent juveniles, just as they do on adults. When it comes to kids who rape, maim and kill, their age quickly becomes unimportant.

For those juveniles who become second offenders, there should be the option of a fixed sentence followed by a conditional release until age twenty-five. I call this career criminal control for troublesome kids.

The conditions for their release from custody would be simple: No arrests, full-time employment or school, and a weekly check-in with the local police precinct. You would *have* to be registered.

7. End parole and probation—not just for kids, for everyone.

In New York, the recidivism rate for juveniles is 75 percent, and the adult rate is close to that. What this tells me is that probation is not working, just as early release programs from prison—which we call parole— are not working. So let us have the courage to change. I am calling for the total elimination of probation and parole as we know it. In their place, probationers and parolees would be required to register at their local precinct and check in each week with a police officer. This would free up billions, and that money could be used to build more jails, to hire more police, to fight crime more intelligently. In time, the local precinct would come to know all the local lawbreakers, and you can imagine the sobering impact this new policy would have on offenders. Community policing is touted by many liberals as the wave of the future—and this would be the ultimate form of community policing. Let us give it a try. What do we have to lose?

8. No more free lawyers, no more free rides.

Too many people treat the juvenile justice system as a joke, especially the parents of kids who get a taxpayer-supported lawyer and lose little sleep over their children's lawbreaking. That would change overnight if we required them to pay for the attorneys who try to keep their kids out of jail. They should pay according to their means, even if it is a percentage of their welfare benefits. I would make them pay for the cost of incarceration as well. Raising children is a parent's responsibility, and if they have screwed up, taxpayers should not shoulder the entire burden. We have thousands of kids in state institutions, and most of them come from homes on public assistance. In too many states, the welfare keeps flowing while the kids are in jail. This is dumber than dumb. Let us not forget middle-class kids: Their parents claim them as tax deductions—even as the state pays for their upkeep in detention facilities. That, too, must end, and the parents must reimburse the state for housing their failures.

Finally, kids should pay for their crimes. Literally. Many communities have laws which permit judges to order financial restitution from delinquents, but few of them are used. I believe in mandatory juvenile restitution, nationwide. It could be funded from work programs when kids are in custody, or from special projects in the community. If you crack somebody's head open, you should pay a price in more ways than one. We are talking about responsibility: cause and effect, pleasure and pain, right and wrong, order and disorder.

CHAPTER 3

Judicial Diversity Doesn't Mean a Mixed Bag of Nuts

Several years ago, Little Richard, the famous rock and roll singer, was seriously injured in a Los Angeles auto crash. He lost control of a sports car while driving at a high rate of speed and smashed into a telephone pole.

The charismatic black entertainer was unconscious when paramedics wheeled him into Cedars-Sinai Medical Center. When he met with reporters several weeks later, Little Richard said he had little or no memory of the auto accident.

"All I remember is waking up in a Jewish hospital

and saying, 'Thank God,'" he told them. "I feel good. I'm just so glad to be alive."

What does this have to do with judges? The answer: Everything.

In family court, judges make life and death decisions every day. We face challenges every bit as daunting as those facing a team of surgeons: Do we return children to their parents? Will they be safe? Was the baby's arm broken during a fall, or did Mom break it in frustration? Do we deny Dad's visitation with his kids because Mom claims he abused them? Do we give a fifteen-year-old robber probation, or are the risks to the community too high?

If judges make mistakes in these and countless other cases, the results can be life threatening. But all too often, justice is denied, largely because of the way we choose our judges in the first place. Too often, these appointments are based not on ability and wisdom, but on political expediency, payback, race, gender and other "politically correct" criteria. That is absurd.

What You Want Is the Best

Little Richard did not seem too concerned when mostly white doctors from a Jewish hospital saved his life. He did not complain that the ambulance team failed to seek out African-American surgeons, and you would not either, faced with such a crisis. What you would want are the best experts available, regardless of skin color or religion, gender or sexual orientation. And if you would not choose a surgical team based on affirmative action, or "cultural diversity," why should the selection of judges be any different?

We have to start scrutinizing trial court and appeals judges and demand accountability. That means opening up courtrooms that are too often shielded from public scrutiny. It means shining a light on serious criminal cases that all too often escape our attention.

In this chapter, I will give you a glimpse of juvenile criminals who laugh at the law when higher courts reverse their convictions. We will meet judges who let derelicts destroy public places, and you can draw your own conclusions about a subway mugger who viciously beat up his victim, then got millions from the police who arrested him.

We pay little attention to judges who give knee-jerk preference to mothers in custody fights, treating fathers like second-class citizens, and who become judicially comatose when they hear the words sex abuse. The suggestions I offer at the end can help us put the system back on track. You be the judge.

Clearly, no one should be excluded from the bench because of race, gender or other characteristics. That would be wrong—and clearly unconstitutional. Brainpower and common sense dictate that experience should be the benchmark, not some misguided fairness which may look and sound good, but smells awfully bad to those litigants who suffer the consequences of a second-rate judiciary. The intelligent, diligent and caring judges who negotiate the judicial system are also diminished by those who lack qualification to preside over the lives of people.

In New York we have trial courts, a midlevel appellate court and the Court of Appeals, which is the highest court in the state. Trial judges generally do not overtly comment on the decisions made by appellate courts, and with very good reason. Would you berate a doctor who is about to perform a colonoscopy?

Some appellate decisions, however, so fail to reflect the reality of our time, they simply must be questioned by both the legal profession and the public. In so doing, it makes you wonder about the qualifications and fundamental smarts of some of these men and women in black.

Years ago, when I was a practicing attorney in family court, it was easy to spot the smart judges, the dumb ones, the diligent judges and the lazy ones. Most of them have gone to judge heaven as of this writing. As a trial judge, however, I do not have the opportunity to view my colleagues at work, and therefore cannot offer my own observations on their day-to-day performance. I must restrict myself to talking about federal and appellate court decisions that have been made public. Believe me, there is no shortage of material.

Closed Courts Protect Lousy Lawyering and Bad Judging

You, the public, should have the right to view all trial court proceedings. Open access should be the rule rather than the exception in courts throughout the country, but too many are closed by the judge's order. That has got to stop. Closed courtrooms offer protections, but not to the public. They protect lousy lawyering, bad judging and ineffective social institutions, and sometimes all three at once.

Take the case of Randy K., thirteen years old, who was arrested and charged with a knifepoint robbery. His mother came to the precinct, and the police released him to Mom, instead of detaining the boy and bringing him directly to court. They gave the two an "appointment" to appear in court on a later day and sent them on their way. Believe it or not, New York law permits this, even after a serious crime has taken place. I am sure Randy's victim was delighted.

Would it surprise you to learn that neither Randy nor his mother appeared to keep their "appointment"? A warrant was issued for the boy's arrest, and he was picked up three months later to face the original charges. But he was paroled again, by another kindly judge, and given another "appointment."

Once again, he failed to appear, so the court issued another warrant. Randy was arrested, this time on another charge, and finally detained for trial.

At this point, the boy's lawyer made a motion to have the original charges dismissed because, he said, his client had not received a speedy trial, which is guaranteed under the Constitution and by the state of New York.

The trial judge, convulsed with laughter at the lunacy of this argument, quickly denied the motion and scheduled a trial for Randy, at which he was convicted of robbery. His lawyer appealed, not on the basis of his guilt or innocence, but because he did not receive a speedy trial. You will not find the result of this appeal in the latest edition of Ripley's, but it belongs there. If you can believe it, New York's highest court reversed Randy's conviction and dismissed the case, even though the delay was caused solely by Randy the Robber.

Fasten your seatbelts, there is more. Four years later, the appeals court used language hauntingly reminiscent of Randy's case in exonerating an adult man charged with attempted murder. The message was that this kind of case will be dismissed unless police diligently deploy their precious resources—at regular intervals—to catch tens of thousands of hiding felons. These are not poor souls languishing behind bars, waiting for trials. They are bouncing around the streets, thumbing their noses at the judges who paroled them, and scoffing at the system's naïveté. They are enjoying the last laugh.

All Aboard—and That Includes the Homeless

Sometimes, bad judging becomes surreal.

Recently, a New York federal judge ruled that Amtrak cannot eject homeless people who are camping out in the railroad terminals. This bizarre decision has profound implications for the millions of people who begin and end each working day by using public transportation. I read this remarkable ruling in my office, which has a great view of New York's new, billion-dollar federal courthouse. I glanced out the window and thought: Instead of putting homeless people in the subways and railroad terminals, perhaps this judge should relocate them to the warm, protected lobbies of the new courthouse. They would be safer there. When it comes to the homeless, we should not cut corners!

Five days after this ruling, the *New York Times* reported that a thirty-eight-year-old woman was assaulted in Pennsylvania Station at eight P.M. by a homeless man who broke her nose in an unprovoked attack. He was apprehended but will no doubt soon be back at home, in the railroad station, long before his victim's nose is realigned. I also wonder about the family of Soon Chin, sixty-three, who was recently pushed to her death in a New York subway station by a homeless man who had a rap sheet two decades long. He, too, has a right to live in the station.

A Criminal-Friendly Criminal Justice System

Our appeals court in New York seems to be in competition with itself to accommodate criminals. Only two justices, regular dissenters, appear to have a firm grasp on reality when it comes to law and order. Here is another example:

Harold Knowings was assaulted and robbed by six thugs in Brooklyn at eleven P.M. He immediately located police and was placed in a police car to help them canvass the area. Soon, he spotted the defendants and pointed them out to the police as his attackers. Case closed, you might think. But no. The lower court convicted Knowings' attackers, and an intermediate appellate court upheld the decision. Yet the state's highest court reversed the conviction, concluding that these men had not received a fair trial.

They noted that the trial judge had refused to hold a pretrial hearing to determine whether the street canvass deprived the defendants of their constitutional rights. Let me explain what this means: If you have a lineup identification, or an identification where the police catch somebody on the street, then bring them to the victim and ask, "Are these the people who robbed you?" the identification procedure must be scrutinized by a court to make sure that it was not biased by police suggestions.

We certainly do not want police to help convict innocent people based on a misidentification. But this case strained the imagination. Never before in the history of jurisprudence has any court said that a street canvass—where there are eight million people, as in New York—should be the subject of a pretrial hearing. Consider the facts: Poor Mr. Knowings was badly beaten up, and when he toured the vicinity in a police car he readily pointed out his attackers, who happened to be walking on the street. How could this be considered suggestive behavior by police? The two dissenters from this decision and the rest of our seasoned trial judges in New York do not understand either. Due process should not be doo-doo process.

When Do the Good Guys Win?

Blind justice should not be dumb justice. Citizens have a right to know about judges like this and take action against them, if so inclined, through the electoral process. When judges cross the sanity line, they should be no less accountable than any other public official. But they are not. Few people pay attention to judicial decisions, and the profession has become isolated from most Americans. That is inexcusable, especially when judges share responsibility for the chaos in our streets and families.

When do the good guys win? In order for the judicial process to maintain public confidence, the outcome of a case should be just. It should reflect common sense. Yet that is not what happened in the case of Robert Ryan.

A man in his twenties, Ryan was convicted of a drug-related crime involving two pounds of hallucinogenic mushrooms. This crime became a felony beause of the weight of the drugs. Pretty standard, you would think. But when the highest court in New York got involved, Mr. Ryan's case took on global proportions. He was convicted in a lower court, but the high court reversed that decision, setting up yet another barrier between the good guys and our judicial system.

Here is how the higher court justified its action: It held, for the first time, that prosecutors must prove beyond a reasonable doubt, not merely that someone possessed drugs, but that they knew the precise weight of the drugs! Apart from being ludicrous on its face, this ruling has now placed hundreds of drug cases on appeal. The mushroom law has now been extended to heroin, cocaine, crack and a whole menu of illegal drugs. Thanks to this ruling, it is not enough to simply catch someone with physical evidence. You have to get inside their heads and prove what they know! Police must also be mind readers.

I wish this was the worst of it, but judges are raising eyebrows all the time. The heralded case of the subway mugger is even harder to believe.

Extra! Court Makes Mugger Millionaire!

Bernard McCummings was caught in the act of robbing Mr. Jerome Sandusky, seventy-two, on a New York subway platform. Fortunately for Mr. Sandusky, a transit officer heard his screams of terror and responded quickly to the scene. Mr. McCummings tried to flee and was shot by the officer. He was paralyzed as a result, and after pleading guilty to armed robbery, the felon turned around and sued the transit authority for his injuries. He was awarded a whopping $4.3 million!

That's $4.3 million charged to taxpayers because a cop did his job. This outrageous verdict was affirmed by our appellate courts.

Earth to appeals court: The public is fed up with criminals. It is bad enough that so many are released back to the streets on absurd legal technicalities. But to make them millionaires is diabolical.

In March of 1995, a state supreme court judge in New York ruled that Mr. Sandusky, who had sued Mr. Mugger for damages, could not prevail in his lawsuit against him. The judge's interpretation of the law precluded such a recovery. If Mr. Mugger had written a book or sold his story to television for $4.3 million, the victim could have collected. But because a New York jury was dumb enough to give Mr. Mugger the money as damages, it was protected from the lawsuit. So much for reason. So much for fair. So much for justice.

The Judicial Hall of Shame Is Crowded

Poor Elizabeth Doe. One night, she reported to police that her boyfriend had assaulted her with a gun. They had begun canvassing the neighborhood looking for the suspect when Ms. Doe spotted Clive Spencer, a friend of the suspect, seated in a double-parked car. The woman told police that he would likely know her boyfriend's whereabouts, and so they approached the car.

Mr. Spencer began driving away, and police stopped his vehicle.

They approached the car with their flashlights on and were able to see a bag of drugs in plain view on the seat. When Mr. Spencer got out of the car, they could also see the butt of a gun protruding from under the driver's seat. The police promptly arrested him, and with good reason. He was convicted in a lower court, but then our court of appeals got into the act once again, dissecting this professional police work.

They reversed his conviction, finding that police had no right to stop his car. Despite the fact that they were investigating an armed felony, despite the fact that they found drugs and an illegal weapon in his car, Mr. Spencer was not legally guilty. The court rationalized that it was all right for police to approach Mr. Spencer's car as long as it was not moving. But once it started to move, they were powerless to stop it. By halting him, they violated his constitutional rights!

In these and other cases, there were strongly worded dissents. While they do not have any legal weight, they lighten the hearts of those people who live and work in the legal trenches, as opposed to those who work in Oz.

Bad Judges Make Bad Law

We can demand reasoned justice from our courts, but we will not get it by complaining and wringing our hands. All of us have to get involved.

Step one is called democracy. Our chief executives and legislators can be fired by the people anytime their politics and direction clash with the will of the majority. But what of the judiciary, that mysterious branch of government that issues sweeping rulings and is too often impervious to logic, reality and the will of the majority? Obviously, we all want to protect judges from the passions of daily politics. We do not want to hire and fire them based on snap opinion polls. But being insulated from politics does not mean being insulated from reality. The first change must come from the people themselves: We all have to become more knowledgable about our judges, who they are and how they decide cases.

With the help of the media, we could keep abreast of the judiciary just as we monitor our legislators. Maybe newspapers could publish columns several times a month about recent court decisions—to inspire debate and to let us know who should be re-elected and who removed at election time.

If a judge consistently authors opinions that people find offensive, then the people can work their will. If judges are appointed, we have to let the appointing authorities know of our displeasure. You cannot just complain and expect to get results. You have to get involved.

Next, all judicial candidates must pass a substantive written test. There are certain qualifications that every prospective judge should have, whether they aspire to service in family, criminal, civil, housing, surrogate or appeals courts. Unless you can pass a fundamental examination of your expertise, you should not even be considered for appointment to the bench.

This would begin to remove some of the politics from our judicial appointment process. If a hack cannot pass a test, he or she is out of luck. If they make the grade, the selection process can go forward. No exceptions. Liking children is nice but does not qualify you to be a family court judge, any more than living in a house qualifies you for housing court.

We might also consider five-year probationary terms for appointed judges, during which the public could watch them, critique them and then decide whether they have the right stuff. After five years, these jurists could be recertified and acquire tenure, maybe for a fifteen-year term. At least we would get a good look at the goods before permanently purchasing the merchandise.

All Good Judges Draw on Their Experience

Being a good judge requires building a fund of knowledge, legal and practical. The law, coupled with common sense, can be powerful. Sometimes it can even save your judicial derriere.

I have always tried to draw on my experiences as a judge so that the right thing happens in each case that I hear. Sometimes, that experience serves me well when I am trying to protect myself. As a new judge in 1982, I was sent on the so-called judicial circuit for a summer to cover for judges who were on vacation. My first assignment was a two-week stint in Kings County Family Court, one of the busiest in the nation. The division I was assigned to handles about two hundred cases a day, and it was quite a learning experience.

After several days, I heard a case involving a man who had violated a family court order of protection. He stood six foot seven and weighed 300 pounds, pure gin and muscle. He came in handcuffed, and bailiffs removed the restraints while I carefully informed him of his rights. I told him he had a right to have a lawyer represent him; that I could assign counsel if he was indigent. He was accused of having assaulted his former girlfriend, the mother of four children, and he faced a six-month sentence.

But the man said, "I don't want no lawyer." I examined his record and it appeared that he was knowledgeable about the criminal justice system, since he had violated court orders of protection on at least three other occasions, always without consequence. I told him that he had the right to a trial on the charges—that he had beaten up his girlfriend in a local grocery by knocking a five-foot display of canned peas on her head. The man glowered at me and said: "I don't need no trial. That bitch ain't gonna humiliate me."

I explained to this gentleman that if he admitted the violation, I was going to sentence him to six months in jail. But he clearly did not believe me, and insisted on graphically describing how he had stalked this woman for days before assaulting her. When he finished his story, I thanked him and ruled that he had, in fact, violated the court order. I then sentenced him to six months in jail. As the court officers attempted to put the handcuffs back on and lead him away, he looked shocked and his eyes grew wild.

"What the hell are you doing?" he shouted.

"You're being taken to jail for six months," an officer answered. "That ain't gonna happen!" the man exploded. "Who did that?"

The officers explained that the judge had sentenced him, and he began shouting that he wanted my name. Actually, he said something like: "I'm gonna cut her fucking heart out! She ain't never gonna see Christmas!" And so on.

Frankly, I was a little frightened. When he demanded to know my name I instructed the court officers to remove his manacles and give him a pencil and paper. I told the man that my name was Huttner. H-U-T-T-N-E-R. Judge Huttner was the supervising judge in Kings County at the time and I made the following rationalization: I was only a visitor. This was his county, his court. I would make my own enemies in due time in my own county. But this baby was his.

Justice Will Prevail—and My Name Is Kaplan

Years later, I drew on this experience. A man came before me after a long trip from an upstate prison. Prosecutors wanted to terminate his rights as the parent of two children, enabling them to be adopted by the foster parents who had been caring for them for years. The man had been serving a twelve-year sentence for manslaughter, and when he strode into my courtroom, his immense size all but blocked out the sunlight.

He looked like he had done nothing else but work out for the past nine years; his muscles had muscles. I assigned him an attorney and adjourned the case for six weeks, so there would be time to prepare his case. The man looked wild and out of control. When court officers returned him to a holding cell for transportation back upstate, they told me the man had shouted that anyone who thought they were going to terminate his parental rights would suffer a grotesque, painful death and blah-blah-blah. I carefully noted this on his file, and ordered my court officer to alert me when his case came up again. I also noted that he had only three more years to go on his sentence.

Now, I have five children and three grandchildren who depend on me for their emotional and, some, for financial support. I suggested to my court officer that the next time this monster came before me, he should run next door, take Judge Kaplan's sign from his bench, and place it prominently in front of me.

Judge Kaplan is a lovely guy—but he's a bachelor! His only relative is an aged mother who hardly needs him for support. I figured I would tell him about this in a couple of years. That would give him time to change his name.

CHAPTER 4

"Let Us Pay" Hasn't Worked; Let's Try "Make Them Pay"

How would you feel if, month after month, your cousin Billy came banging on the door asking for money? There is nothing wrong with him, and he is clearly able to work and support himself. He is just the family sponge, and nobody has had the guts to tell him to shape up. How long would it take before you hung a big sign on your front door saying GONE SOUTH—FOREVER? Most folks would bail out cousin Billy once or twice, and that would be it. Who in their right mind would keep giving him handouts?

Sounds reasonable. But what would you say to total strangers who make demands, week after week, in ever larger amounts, all over this country?

That is what our welfare system has become, and while politicians come and go with promises of reform, little has been done to revise the rules for public assistance in the United States. We all pay for this—through the nose.

Welfare Is Charity

Even though some folks do work hard to avoid responsibility for their lives, welfare is not a job. They expect taxpayers to pick up the tab, and we do not discourage them.

The dictionary defines charity as "generosity and helpfulness, especially toward the needy or suffering." The needy or suffering. Not deadbeats or chiselers. It is not supposed to be for people like cousin Billy, who would remain a dependent man-child until he sucks his final breath.

America is a compassionate country, but its pockets are not bottomless. Responsibility begins at home, and families must act responsibly before seeking the largesse of strangers. Before I hear a knee-jerk chorus of how our country is one big caring family, let me ask you two simple questions: Aren't you tired of people who always have their hands out and do little to improve their lives? Isn't it time we changed the rules—once and for all?

Those who argue that the majority of people on welfare are short-term, recently unemployed and otherwise responsible folks are missing the point. These are the people for whom welfare protection was designed, and there is every reason to give them a hand. But the problem is those millions of others who are consuming billions of welfare and other entitlement dollars from one generation to the next, and contributing little or nothing to America. We have permitted and tacitly encouraged welfare dependency to become a lifestyle, rather than a safety net.

Individuals are supposed to take care of themselves. Parents should take pride in their ability to support and nurture children. Yet somehow, this once firmly held belief got lost in the past forty years, and the welfare community now operates on radically different assumptions. In its precincts, responsibility is a dirty word.

What follows is a ground-zero view of the welfare mess. The reality of welfare is often quite different from political debates and media portrayals. It is a world of fast-buck artists, dishonesty and high-level scamming. It is also a place where some people legitimately try to get off the dole and live productive lives, with only mixed results. In either case, the system is failing badly and we are all the worse for it.

Teenage pregnancy is a big part of the welfare problem, and it is time for some tough solutions. Being a parent means being responsible, and that applies not only to teenage mothers and fathers, but to their parents. If your kids are having kids, and they wind up on welfare, you as parents must pitch in and help defray the public costs.

Finally, we need to lower the boom on welfare cheats as never before. Through a national media campaign and stronger law enforcement, we should at least try to end the rip-offs and frauds once and for all. Far too many people are swelling the rolls through dishonesty and waste, and to those folks who think the government owes them a living on welfare, my answer is—the government owes you nothing.

Only Disabled in America

Tino, a forty-year-old man with a muscular build, came to New York from Puerto Rico about twelve years ago. He has been on welfare ever since. In Puerto Rico, he told me, he had been a maintenance worker and supported his family. But once in Manhattan, he had developed asthma, which prevented him from working.

Well, I asked him, if you felt better in Puerto Rico and could work for a living, why don't you go back? He looked at me as if I was crazy.

Maybe I am. I have heard similar hard-luck stories from people who came to America from Russia, Pakistan, the Dominican Republic and other countries. They have mastered the dole, and they are not about to give up a steady stream of welfare checks if they can avoid it. Why work for a living?

I keep returning to the story of cousin Billy. We should think of America as we think of our own home. When relatives fall on hard times, you take them in until they get on their feet. If they are sincere and hardworking, they are anxious to get their lives back together and make their own way. But if they are like Billy, they will eat your food and deplete your family's income day after day, month after month, until there is nothing left.

At first, you feel sympathetic and generous. Then you get angry.

Whatever happened to self-reliance and pride? Most of us grew up with these values, and we have tried to impart them to our kids. One of my five children, for example, loves to have babies and she is a great mother. Jamie is a natural nurturer, and she is married to a lovely guy who struggles to make ends meet for his family on a cop's salary. I love her dearly, and I love my grandchildren more than life itself. But I have told her repeatedly: Do not have more kids than you can afford to raise. This is not unreasonable or cruel. It is merely responsible, and most Americans know this without being told.

If we can face these truths in our own homes, why do some morons complain when society tells welfare recipients to stop having babies whom they cannot support? I do not want to support my daughter's children, and I *love* her. Why would I want to support children conceived irreverently and irresponsibly by a bunch of strangers?

Dole Dependency Diminishes Development

The consequences of this unwanted baby boom are everywhere:

Teenage pregnancy leads to welfare reliance, and that is often a precursor to drug addiction, child abuse, child neglect, domestic violence, lack of self-esteem and hopelessness. If you infantilize an entire segment of the population in the name of charity, families are destroyed. Unless we discourage people from having kids they cannot care for—both financially and emotionally—we will keep our gargantuan social service bureaucracies, including family courts, straining to keep pace. We will keep the social service agencies that shore up the family courts in business, as well as the bureaucrats who grow fat off other people's misery. And the people who will suffer most are the unwanted children themselves, the innocents.

Let us get back to basics: Welfare is charity, something we freely give—or choose not to give—to the truly needy. It is not a job. When people come before me in family court, I often ask if and how they support themselves. The vast majority tell me that *they* support themselves and their children. And when I ask what they do for a living, they usually reply, "I'm on welfare." To them, it is their job.

It's as if in America we encourage irresponsible behavior. Every new welfare baby means some parent or parents are getting a larger check. The men and women supported by our public charity should not be having more children and expecting the American family to pay the tab. They should not be having additional kids whom they cannot possibly support. Those who do so—and there are millions of them across the country—are stealing from the public's checking account. Their mistakes cannot continue to be our emergency.

Some states have given them the green light to steal. Consider Massachusetts, which had actually offered fertility counseling to people on welfare. Can anything be dumber? Who was the genius who dreamed up that policy? I cannot believe the majority of taxpayers in that state supported this harebrained scheme, because it violates all common sense. But apparently people stay up nights dreaming of ways to fleece the taxpayers.

Having a Baby Is Easy; Being a Parent Is Hard

You cannot be a good father if you have two kids with Bertha, one with Diane, three in the Dominican Republic and one in Ohio. I see men like this all the time in court, but they are not parents. They are irresponsible procreators, and they cost us a bundle.

Most thinking people do not condone welfare recipients who are double-dipping or otherwise cheating at taxpayers' expense. That is a fraud and a crime. But an equally insidious problem that has repercussions in the very social fabric of our culture is that there is less marriage these days among the public assistance population, and it has nothing to do with some philosophical taboo. It has to do with economics. Benefits and money are tied to a marriage license, and those homes where the mother and father are legally married stand to get far less from taxpayer-supported programs.

Countless people have opted for "alternative lifestyles" to pull in more monthly benefits. They refuse to get married, even though the men are actually living in the same home as the women. In doing so they make a mockery of any family responsibility. I see hundreds of people like this every week. They have learned that by not marrying, the men can work—usually off the books—and women can get more benefits as their children multiply. Meanwhile, the taxpayers shell out money for housing, food, clothing and medical care.

How do we solve this problem?

One solution would be to bring back common-law marriage. This would mean that we consider a man and woman married if they establish a family and live under the same roof. It might stall the welfare gravy train for many freeloaders. They could not have perks without real responsibilities. We have heard a lot about the dignity of alternative lifestyles, and I believe that any lifestyle that does not drain the public purse should be recognized—unless the object of that lifestyle is to defraud the public.

You cannot demand responsible behavior from people if you don't know who they are. And when mothers on welfare refuse to name the fathers of their children—so that the courts can recoup the public monies expended on behalf of their children—public welfare benefits should be either denied or deferred until these elusive fathers are tagged. Ducking that responsibility is one of the biggest scams in the welfare community, and it should stop now. By targeting these fathers, we would be able to recoup financial support from them, and finally make them pay for their families. They may not cover the entire bill, but they might think twice about making another dependent if the dependent was theirs, not ours.

Getting Over on the System Is an Art Form

Many of these men have learned that the easiest way to duck responsibility is to hide their income, while the public pays. But we should send them a message that this hide-and-seek game will not be tolerated. If you are a parent who is not paying child support, you should not be able to buy a home, get a credit card or receive a passport. This would apply equally to people who are either getting paychecks or are self-employed. In each case, the federal government should order an IRS audit of anyone who is delinquent in child support payments. In virtually every home, a letter from the IRS is about as welcome as the bride at a bachelor party.

Deadbeat dads are a national disgrace, but the problem of welfare and children goes even deeper. Every day in family court I see teenage girls with children. I deal with eighteen-year-olds who have three or four children, and are pregnant with yet another. How do we discourage them from having more?

The first step is to deal with their parents. These mothers and fathers, whoever they are, should be responsible for the support of their children's children—until they reach the age of twenty-one or become self-supporting. And that does not apply just for the teenage mother's parents. The parents of a teenage boy who cannot keep his pants on should have a similar responsibility.

If we set up these legal requirements, we would suddenly have up to six people—a mother, father, plus maternal and paternal grandparents—expected to support additional children. And by this I mean cost-bearing as well as child-rearing. If responsibility started in the home, where it surely belongs, I strongly believe that our welfare birth rates would go down.

Carmen was seventeen when she got pregnant with her second child by Jose, who was sixteen. Carmen's mother was disgusted and told her daughter that she would no longer tolerate such conduct. She insisted that Carmen terminate the second pregnancy, or she would throw her out of the house. But Jose's mother, a working lady, welcomed Carmen into their home. She then filed a custody petition for both Carmen and her infant. This enabled her, according to the system, to receive welfare benefits for both Carmen and her children.

Think how different it would be if this paternal grandmother had to bear the support of these two children herself, rather than with public funds. I wonder how quickly she would have volunteered her home? Perhaps her son would have been better off with some counseling or good old-fashioned discipline. What he needed was a lesson in birth control. At least the grandmother would not be able to make us foot the bill for these mistakes, and they *are* mistakes, not "little blessings."

There is not much we can do with the children who are already receiving public assistance. The idea is to make it painful for kids considering having more kids. It is time to stop funding one program after another to help teenage mothers, as if this were a national priority. The only message these programs send is that we accept girls having one baby, or two or three. So let us change the message.

What we have been doing clearly has not worked. Often, teenage pregnancy leads to other pathologies. Other babies follow, families become dysfunctional, children are neglected, domestic violence erupts, and custody feuds rage on and on. The kids themselves look miserable. I know from my professional experience that their future is bleak.

Without developing self-reliance, these young women will continue to justify their lives by having more kids. How do you encourage, guide or force someone to be self-reliant? The cries of the lame liberal left about the paucity of day care resulting in the inability of these women to work again are not really on target. Self-reliance means reliance on oneself, not the government. Let four welfare mothers get tegether: One is the designated day care provider, paid by the wages of the other three. Call it co-op day care. It should be the national model.

There is nothing wrong with asking the grandmothers and grandfathers of these babies to lend a hand. They should baby-sit, while Mom or Dad goes out in the working world and learns something about financial responsibility. Then, Mom or Dad can baby-sit while Grandma or Grandpa works. If you are old enough to have a baby, you are old enough to pack groceries after school. If you are old enough to bring a child into the world, you should be able to clean a house. If your mother has not done an adequate job of teaching family responsibility, she can at least help out with day care. The answer lies in the home. Enough programs!

Lower the Boom on Welfare Cheats

I have seen parents collecting public assistance payments for kids who are in jail and even for kids who are dead. I have seen people continue to collect checks while they work off the books, as livery cab drivers or at the local bodega. Some of them make a lot more money than I do, by selling drugs. It takes some nerve to turn around and seek additional taxpayer funds—welfare—to help pay for your children.

We need a national campaign to crack down on such abuse, because the system is clearly incapable of reforming itself. No governmental authority will ever be able to root out welfare fraud without such outside help. Bureaucrats do not really care about these problems, because solving them only makes their lives more complicated. This, then, is what we must do.

Starting immediately, government declares a welfare amnesty for sixty days. Anyone receiving public funds who is not entitled to them would have sixty days to close their fraudulent public assistance accounts, no questions asked, no penalties assessed. After that, courts should lower the boom. Federal, state and local prosecutors, boosted by political officials and a nationwide media campaign, should launch an all-out war on welfare fraud. Jail would be mandatory.

Some will say this is too cruel. But I ask you—what else has worked? What existing policy has brought common sense to our costly welfare programs?

Equal Opportunity Inconvenience

It is clear to me that, as disgusted as Americans may be about paying for these kids, nobody is going to let them starve. Threats of cutting off welfare payments for new babies born to teenage welfare mothers have no bite. They are only bark.

But what if we tapped into the welfare payments received by fathers and mothers to pay for their children? When I had more children as a working mother, nobody gave *me* a raise. I had to make do with what I had. I spent less on myself so I'd have more to provide for the kids, and so should welfare families.

Teenagers having children are the beginning of a process that only has a downside. These kids can hardly negotiate their own lives, and are surely in no position to care emotionally or financially for a child. But teens are having kids in bumper numbers and in the vast majority of cases, the taxpayers are footing the bill.

Most of the teenage parents I see are on their parents' welfare budget. The teen mother lives at home with her mother and the teen father with his. Why not cut the welfare budgets of both families proportionately to pay for each new baby? We would do it firmly but fairly and the message would be clear: Every new baby brings responsibility. The primary responsibility for keeping teenagers in check is with their parents. If you as parents have failed, the financial burden should not rest solely with the taxpayers. Is this too harsh? I think not. It may be inconvenient and that is precisely the point. Let us call it equal opportunity inconvenience.

At the very least, we could put an end once and for all to the notion that bringing more welfare babies into the world is somehow a demonstration of manly prowess. Some young men clearly don't get the message and it's time we reached them loud and clear.

Recently, I grilled a young father in my court who had been arrested for a minor infraction. He was barely nineteen, and told me that he had just visited two girlfriends in the same maternity ward who had given birth to two daughters—each his own! Proud and arrogant, he was bragging, as if life was one big fertility rite. Both children, naturally, were new welfare recipients. This is some America.

Several days later, I encountered another class act, this time a man who was seeking visitation rights for three children. He stood on one side of the courtroom, and three welfare mothers—each with a different child—stood on the other! The children were all born out of wedlock, and they were all on public assistance. This jobless Don Juan was demanding his rights.

I felt it would be unseemly to handle all three cases

together, so I established his paternity (or fatherhood) one at a time. Each time, in response to his request for visitation, I asked how much he was paying to support his new child. "Nothing," he replied. "I ain't working."

Next, I asked the man, thirty-two, when the last time he had held a job was, and he said it was at least two years ago. How did he support himself? "I live at home, with my mom," he answered. How does she support herself? "She's on SSI," he answered. Leaning forward, I asked if there was anything wrong with him, and then he got quite angry. What did I mean by such a question?

"Well, sir," I replied, "is there any reason why you're thirty-two years old, the picture of health, and you don't work?" The man glowered, and said he couldn't find anything he liked to do. "Well," I answered, "from the three paternity cases here today, there clearly is something you very much like to do. It is just too bad that you can't make a living at it."

The Nine Lives of Deadbat Dads

When men fall delinquent in child support payments, the system gives them chance after chance, delay after delay. All the while, their children go without the necessities of life. Or the public pays. Very often I have found that the only way to get money out of these fathers is to threaten them not only with jail, but with the sound of handcuffs. Once they hear these magic clicks, it is surprising how quickly the money that is not there suddenly appears.

For the truly hard-core, an hour or two in our not-so-attractive detention cells works like a charm. As these derelict fathers are led away, I often tell my court officers to whisper that in civil jail—where these men are going—the inmates dig graves for elephants. That is usually all it takes before I see the color of green, and hear loud promises of instant reform.

The welfare system is overrun with this problem, but avoidance of child support crosses all economic lines. The middle-class play this game, too. Several years ago, a very affluent physician named Dr. Jones (only the name has been changed, to protect the guilty) was identified as the biological father of a little boy whose mother was struggling to support herself and her son. She had been working two jobs and somehow managed to pay a part-time baby-sitter. Meanwhile, the good doctor had avoided paying child support for eighteen months. The judge who originally handled his case had retired—not a moment too soon, I might add—and so the matter was referred to me. Weeks later, Dr. Jones and his lawyer appeared in court. He had not paid a penny for the boy so far, and had no intention of beginning now. But I quickly disabused him of the notion that this would be business as usual, and informed him that he had three days to come up with $15,000 in back payments. The lawyer and his client still looked unfazed, and left court.

Three days later, with no check, I issued a warrant for the doctor's arrest, and personally called in the warrant squad. I wanted them to execute an arrest warrant immediately, at the doctor's office. Soon, the marshal called me from the doctor's place of business, saying the gentleman could not come to court. He had told the marshal that people would undoubtedly die if he left his offices that day! I told the marshal this was mere speculation, adding that if he did not produce the doctor right away, I could guarantee at least one death. His.

Some forty minutes later, Dr. Jones arrived in court, followed by his attorney. Outrageous! the lawyer said. What unprofessional conduct! he blustered. How dare the city remove Dr. Jones in handcuffs from his office!

I was unmoved, and handed the physician over to our commissioner of corrections. The price of his release? Payment of $15,000 in cash for child support. Within the hour, the money was in court, and the doctor had learned a valuable lesson. Henceforth, his child support payments were made on a regular basis—not on the first of the month, but on the thirtieth of the preceding month. Dr. Jones never wanted to see me again, and his game was over. We had won.

Child support, by the way, means Mom as well as Dad. Several years ago, Josh and Ilene came to court. Josh was requesting visitation rights for their one-year-old son, and also seeking to establish paternity.

Ilene was sixteen, he was twenty, and neither of them were rocket scientists. Yet they were trying to live decent lives. Neither was abusing drugs, and they had never been in jail. They were two irresponsible kids who had a baby while they were both living at home with parents. While Josh worked, Ilene and the baby were on welfare.

I asked Ilene what she did for a living, and she told me that she went to school three days a week, on Monday, Wednesday and Thursday. What did she do the rest of the week? Nothing, Ilene said, adding that she was not opposed to visitation rights for Josh. He was, in fact, paying $25 a week for the child from his job as a bike messenger.

But what about Mom? She, too, had a responsibility to support this child. So I made an order of visitation, giving Josh time with his child each weekend, from Friday through Sunday evenings. Meanwhile, I told Ilene that while Dad had the baby she had to go out and get a job, waiting on tables, or working fast food lines, anything to be productive and contribute to the support of her baby. My plan was to keep them both too busy and too tired to contemplate another bundle.

Mothers Don't Just Make Children; They Have to Support Them, Too

We often forget that. For all our talk about uncooperative dads, it is important to remember that the only difference between a deadbeat father and a deadbeat mother is a nine-month gestation period. Most of these young mothers that I see on welfare are not Mary Poppins; they are not instilling any kind of a work ethic or education ethic in their children, and they are only marginally nurturing these youngsters.

They are teaching their children nothing, and unless they are forced to become more self-reliant—and I do mean forced—they will continue to labor under the misconception that when you have a baby, somebody else pays. Those habits have been ingrained over a lifetime, and it is no surprise that the child who grows up in a welfare household learns nothing about adult responsibility.

If You Don't Like the Rules, Don't Take the Money

Last spring, my husband and I walked to a local restaurant for dinner after a very hard day in court. As we neared the diner, a bedraggled looking woman standing on the corner held out an empty coffee cup and asked me for money. She said she was hungry and needed help.

On impulse, I walked into a luncheonette and ordered her a tuna-fish sandwich and a cup of coffee. I had them put the food in a bag, went outside and handed it to the woman. Naively, I expected some appreciation for this gesture, but the woman snapped: "What's this?"

I told her it was a sandwich and coffee, whereupon she grabbed the package, tossed it into the street and said: "Keep your fucking food." Food for the stomach was clearly not her object. This lady simply wanted money to get high, and I was not prepared to subsidize her habit. I told her so, and walked off.

Day after day, I see similar cases in family court. Women come before me with multiple children, all on welfare. They are charged with neglecting their children by failing to provide food, housing or clothing. Yet we have been giving them welfare checks, food stamps and rent money. Obviously this taxpayer money is going somewhere and it is not to support a home or care for the children. So how do we change this?

Welfare is designed to provide only for the basics of life. To ensure that these basics are provided, why not create a new way to dispense these tax dollars? Instead of paying cash for rent, checks could be sent directly to landlords. A similar voucher might be devised for utilities, which could be cashed only by the utility service. Cash-coded government cards could strictly regulate expenditures on food, as well as basic clothing purchases.

This way, we would ensure that money designed for children and families is used for those purposes, and does not disappear into a crack dealer's pockets.

Liberal critics will say this is demeaning, but I think starving children and neglected infants are far more important than a welfare recipient's ego or sensibilities. If they do not like the rules, let them work for a living.

One of the worst legacies of our welfare system is the idea that recipients have a long list of entitlements. I do not think public largesse entitles you to anything more than a helping hand from taxpayers. After that, you are on your own. Unfortunately, some folks think they are entitled to a lot more.

Like apartments in the big city, in the neighborhood of their choice.

"I'll Take Manhattan . . ."

One morning a young lawyer ran into my courtroom looking pretty frazzled.

She told me that on her train ride in from Queens, where she lived, some derelict had pawed and fondled her in a crowded subway car. Because there was no room to move, she had to endure this groping pervert for nearly five minutes. The attorney confided that she would love to live in Manhattan and be closer to her job, but said she could not afford the rents on her salary.

Fifteen minutes later, a case was called in which this attorney was representing a mother who had successfully completed a residential drug program. She had been looking for a suitable apartment for the previous two months, and her lack of housing was the sole reason her children were still in foster care.

I asked the caseworker why it had taken the woman so long to find an apartment, and she replied that the mother refused to live anywhere other than Manhattan. There were affordable apartments in the city's other boroughs, but this woman—on welfare and cut off from her children—knew what she wanted.

I grew up in Brooklyn and always dreamed of living in Manhattan someday. I had the same dream when I began working in the Bronx, and it was not until I was forty-five years old that I was able to save up enough money to afford a home in Manhattan. I worked hard to get to that point, as have so many other New Yorkers. So where did this mother get off insisting that she *had* to live in the most expensive borough, in the most expensive city in the United States?

By what right? And on whose money? The irony was that the lawyer, fresh from her groping experience that morning, failed to see the bizarre connection between her real estate plight and that of the client standing before us. She leaped to her feet when I asked the woman why she had to live in Manhattan and said: "She has a constitutional right to live wherever she wants."

To which I replied: "Not on my money, she doesn't!"

Charity for the Needy—All Others Get a Job

When I was sitting in Bronx Family Court in the 1980s, there was one division that dealt only with child support. The Bronx is a fascinating borough of New York, because nearly everybody who lived in this community and appeared before me was either unemployed or paid in cash off the books. Nobody wanted to admit that they had a job! Most said with a straight face that despite persistent efforts, they simply could not find gainful employment and were unable to pay child support.

Obviously many thought I had "stupid" written on my forehead. So I began to drive to work taking a different route each morning. I would stop periodically and jot down notes on every establishment that had a sign in the window reading "help wanted." There were many bodegas and livery cab services in need of help. Each day I would have a list of job opportunities fresh and ready for distribution. And every time I heard the refrain—"I can't find any work, Your Honor"—I pulled out my trusty list, ready to help some mother or father earn money to start supporting a family.

One day, a militant gentleman took great exception to my job referral program. He accused me of genocide for suggesting that he take a job with a livery cab company. These drivers were getting killed all the time, he complained, and I should be more concerned about his safety. "I think you're right, sir," I answered. "So don't *drive* livery cabs. *Wash them.*" I promptly gave him the address of a car wash two blocks from the courthouse, and the stunned look on his face said it all. At long last, he was going to enter the workforce . . . just like anybody else.

CHAPTER 5

Foster Care Fiasco

As a mother, there were hair-tearing times when I wished that my daughter would grow up and have a girl "just like her." She is married now and my first grandchild was a boy. But the die was cast, and my wishes were fulfilled years ago. He is every bit the brat she was as a child.

Sometimes she threatens to pack him up and ship him to me as retribution. Mine and his. If she did, should the public pay me for raising him? Sounds ridiculous. Well, hold on to your hats—and your wallets.

In our society, the state can remove kids from their homes if their parents are dysfunctional. It is the state's obligation to consider and protect the welfare of these children. But where do we put these young-sters? Usually with marginal family members or with strangers who are clueless about child rearing. We call it foster care, and it is an outrage.

Let us begin with some disturbing statistics:

The nationwide bill for the more than 460,000 children in foster care exceeds $10 billion annually. If the Child Welfare Agency in New York City could locate all their cases—which they cannot—we would find about 55,000 kids in foster care in this city alone. The entire state of California has 87,000 children in foster care.

Typically, children come into the foster care system in one of three ways. Some have been abused by their parents, others have been neglected, and a lesser number are put in foster care voluntarily by their parents. Once in the system, they can be placed with non-related foster parents, with relatives in so-called kinship foster care or in group homes and other institutions.

All of these foster care efforts are administered by public or private bureaucracies, sometimes both, and despite a decade of billion-dollar budgets, the children are in worse shape than they were before we emptied our pockets to pay for these programs.

For years, Americans have had a stereotypical view of foster care parents as generous, compassionate people who voluntarily take children into their homes and raise them with loving care. There are undoubtedly people like that all across this country, and they deserve our thanks and respect.

Indeed, the purpose of the foster care system is to provide children with a caring environment until they can be safely reunited with biological parents or a permanent plan for their future is set. But the reality is usually quite different.

As you read the following pages, try to imagine a world where brain surgeons and high-priced lawyers work without college degrees or professional certification. We wouldn't stand for it, but most states are quite willing to hand young children over to anyone who calls himself or herself a foster parent.

We compound the problem with boondoggle programs that, in effect, encourage parents to abandon their children and "pay" grandparents thousands of extra dollars to act like grandparents. Meanwhile, nonprofit agencies hop on the foster care gravy train, forcing taxpayers to dig deeper in their pockets.

You won't hear me calling for new programs, because we need less political intervention in family life, not more. How about some commonsense changes, though, like limitations on the time a child can be placed in foster care, and proof of minimal competency before the state gives someone money to raise a stranger's children?

Read on, and get a glimpse of America's foster care fiasco.

Foster Parents Should Be Literate

The typical foster parent I see is a single woman who has several biological children of her own. She is supported by welfare or social security disability. She is a high school dropout whose own kids are marginally functioning. She does not have the ability to help them with their schoolwork, and she has little hope for a brighter economic or social future.

So what do we do? We give her two more children. And why? Because she is available and has no criminal record. To shoulder this added burden, we give her an extra thousand dollars a month or more in tax-free dollars.

That, in a nutshell, is the system. And it is no way to raise kids.

Why not require that prospective foster parents meet a national standard? They must be able to read, write, and spell, plus show some knowledge of basic history and mathematics. They would have to pass a basic intelligence and parenting test and only then would we entrust them with such a precious resource. Only then would we give them public funds, for which they should pay a percentage of taxes, like anyone else.

This way, we might bring foster parents into the mainstream. They would establish credit and, by professionalizing foster parenting, enter the workforce.

What's More Important—Your Toenails or Your Kids?

How many times have you heard someone say, "There ought to be a license to become a parent"? Well, think about it. We license everything from driving a car to giving a pedicure. Yet anyone who reaches puberty is eligible to have a child, whether biological or foster. While our Constitution prevents us from requiring parents to get a license, we can at least ensure that kids once neglected by their biological parents will not be neglected again by the state while in foster care.

Every year in every state a commission meets to attempt to identify the scores of children killed and maimed while in foster care. And each year a report is published with suggestions for legislative and systemic change. Although the number of victims is increasing, there has been no nationwide overhaul of the systems that permit these in-house tragedies to recur.

Most of the victims are minority children. And representatives of the minority community have a legitimate beef here. All it took to overhaul New York's adoption process was the brutal 1988 death of Lisa Steinberg, the pseudo-adopted child of upper-middle-class professional white parents. Suddenly, after a flood of bad publicity, the legislative process kicked into gear. Safeguards were instituted and reforms were under way. Ironically, the Steinberg case was a private adoption gone awry, by all accounts an isolated snafu. But what about the scores of nonwhite children killed and maimed by a social policy that places troubled kids in the homes of abusive or neglectful foster parents? We have not tackled the problem head-on, and the casualties continue to mount.

At the very least, foster parents must demonstrate basic parenting skills.

The single mothers who take on added kids often have no work ethic and little education. We should insist that they have at least a high school diploma and then some mandatory continuing education to maintain their license as caregivers. We should give them written and practical tests and six months of parenting training, with quality control and performance evaluations. Mandatory drug testing for *all* prospective foster parents is essential.

Now, I am certainly not lobbying for big, expensive new federal programs. But these strict new standards—enforced locally—should be a prerequisite for foster parenting.

Maturing Is More Than Just Getting Old

Consider the case of Beatrice Carver, age fifty-three. She had five children and had never been married. Her children were all grown; none were self-supporting and two were in jail. When she came before me, she had two foster care children. The city was conducting a "preadoption" study to assess the suitability of her home. There was not a scintilla of information to suggest that any children placed in her custody were likely to thrive or prosper.

Ms. Carver told the caseworker that she loved little children, yet that hardly gave me confidence in her parenting. There was no way to tell whether she had matured or just grown older. The only thing that had grown was her income—which ballooned from $412 a month from welfare to $2,000 a month from foster care, when she took in two children. These payments would continue if she adopted them, because under our system Ms. Carver would be legally entitled to the money until the children turned twenty-one. Most people think that an adoption ends state support of children. Nothing could be further from the truth. The money continues!

In this case, as with countless others, judges are left with no viable option. The children in this case had been in her care for years before the adoption petition was filed. To remove them from this marginal caregiver would doubtless result in emotional trauma for the children. Even if I did remove them, where would they go? There was no assurance that a better place was waiting for them. I granted the adoption petition because it was the only realistic alternative. Judges are forced to make these decisions every day, but we go home each night and begin the next day renewed. There is no new beginning for these children, and it must change.

Ideally, foster care should promote the growth of healthy and productive kids. That rarely happens, and the reason is that we fail to give these children the right kind of parental role models. Encouraging more adults with strong work and education ethics to become foster parents would be a beginning.

Yet how do we do that without spending a fortune? Here are some ideas:

1. We could offer a tax credit of $10,000 per child for foster parents.
2. The state could subsidize the entire cost of college tuition in a public institution for kids adopted through the foster care system.
3. Insurance companies could be required to cover foster care children for medical coverage on their foster parents' policy.

As I see it, the only new expense would be to provide public day care for all preschool foster children where a demonstrated need exists. Other than that, these foster homes would be totally responsible for a child's needs.

To launch this program, we might mount a national public awareness campaign through the media, one that would hopefully touch the heart and conscience of responsible Americans. If we succeed, we would awaken them to the realization that the only way these children of poverty and neglect can ever become productive adults is by living with a family of productive adults.

A Bed for a Child Is Not Enough

Caregivers should be role models. That is what you and I do for our children, so why expect anything less for society's most at-risk children? Encouraging welfare recipients to take in foster kids is ludicrous. These folks have a hard enough time negotiating their own lives; the last thing they need or should have is a foster child.

While we are at it, we should impose a strict maximum time period for foster care unless there are extraordinary circumstances. If the state has taken your kids because you are a drug addict, one year is more than sufficient time to pull yourself together. After a year, you lose your children to strangers through adoption, or to relatives by custody or guardianship awards. The rights of the child to a secure home overshadow your privileges as a parent. But the more typical cases, where foster care drags on for years with little or no supervision, are wasteful and dangerous for many children. We put them in limbo, then wonder why today's foster kids become tomorrow's problem adults.

Kinship Foster Fraud

The virus of fraudulent foster care plagues communities across America, but in recent years a new strain has developed that is even more pernicious. It is called "kinship foster care," and it deserves its own wing in the Hall of Scams. The people who dreamed it up may have thought they were giving unlucky kids a break—but they have created a monster.

Kinship foster care began in New York ten years ago. It was designed to keep neglected or abused children with their extended families, and to give enhanced cash stipends to relatives—usually grandmothers and aunts—who took them in. In other words, if Mom or Dad failed to provide proper care, the state paid Grandma to give her grandchildren a better home.

Since then, the program has spread across the country. In theory, kinship foster care is beneficial to child development by keeping kids in a familiar setting. Clearly, children feel less stigmatized in a relative's home. We know this from years of experience with so-called informal adoptions, where extended family members took care of one another's children, free of government subsidies and oversight.

But today, this practice has evolved into something radically different. It has become a runaway train, consuming vast amounts of tax dollars. Relatives quickly learned about this new money pot, and demanded entry into the foster care club. It is preventing us from monitoring the care all children receive, because of the strain of the sheer numbers of kids now in the system.

Children placed with relatives usually remain in the foster care system for longer periods of time. The parents from whom they were removed often have free access to relatives' homes and with all that money coming into the family from taxpayers, there is little incentive to work toward reunification. Therefore, as more children enter foster care through the front door, fewer kids leave the system, and the numbers swell.

Kinship foster care is the latest rage in social service circles, but it creates a raft of serious problems. The lure of tax-free dollars, for example, creates a disincentive to family reunification, since the monthly foster care stipends are triple or quadruple those of public assistance.

It Pays to Keep the Family Apart

I used to think that grandparents had a sacred obligation to their grandchildren, a blood commitment that transcended all other obligations. I guess I am old-fashioned. Go ask Alice, a fifty-three-year-old grandmother who is raising three grandchildren. She undertook this responsibility because of her daughter's irresponsibility. But nobody told her about the extra foster care money she could be getting from the state: "I only get their welfare money. We are the state's baby-sitters," she complains. "The state pushes children on grandparents. If the state is going to do that, pay us for it."

Maybe she thinks her daughter sprang from spontaneous generation. You raised her, Alice.

Consider the case of a New York grandmother who takes in her four grandchildren because Mom is a crack addict who lives on the street. If two of these children are considered "special needs" youngsters, they are entitled to maximum benefits. This grandmother, herself a welfare recipient, gets $3,200 per month to care for these children—tax- and account-ability-free. She still lives in the same government-subsidized housing and pays $138 a month in rent. When her daughter drops by to visit the kids, she scrounges a few extra bucks for drugs and then disappears again. The money continues to pour in.

No wonder kinship foster care is one of the more popular new social service programs in low-income communities. It has grown rapidly: Almost half the children in foster care in New York and California are enrolled, and since these kids are cared for by a familiar family member, there is less incentive for the parents of these children to straighten up, so the kids often remain in technical foster care forever.

Indeed, these families have more money than ever, and parents are often able to visit their children whenever they like. Since quality casework is almost nonexistent, I suspect that many "unfit" parents continue to live in these households. The last caseworker I ordered to make an unannounced visit to a grandmother's home found no grandma. But she did find the new baby—who had been born drug-addicted—in bed with her stoned-out mother.

We'll Terminate Your Rights—but Not Your Responsibilities

Other abuses take place when parents simply dump their kids. Their financial responsibility ends once their legal rights are terminated. The game can get out of hand, but there is a way to stop it:

If adoption is the ultimate solution for these kids, let us keep wandering parents on the hook for financial reimbursements of whatever money the state spends on their children. Call it split adoptions. Maybe the only remaining link between a biological parent and child would be financial, but we would send the message that you cannot just walk away from parental responsibilities. One way or another, it is going to cost you.

During a recent trial, a father happily agreed to the termination of his parental rights to two teenage boys. They were living with his sister, a kinship foster parent. I began questioning the caseworker about the father, who did not even bother to show up for a second hearing—he was working. I learned that Dad was content that his sister had agreed to adopt his boys; they were all living in the same building. He had started a new family and could hardly be expected to support *all* his children!

He saw his boys daily but bore no financial responsibility for them. To ensure his continued freedom from any fiscal obligations, he was readily consenting to this intrafamily adoption. His sister was to receive $1,100 per month net for the boys from the state until they were twenty-one years old.

I was appalled at this legal fiction and dismissed the petition. Any other result violated the very spirit of our adoption laws and would perpetrate a fraud on the public and the courts. This man was a hustler, clearly out to beat the system and avoid his duty as a father.

Unfortunately, the city—always ready to shoot itself in the foot—and the lawyer for the man's two children quickly appealed my decision to our appellate court. At first, the court ruled that I was correct, saying that the adoption would be fraudulent and a sham. But then, months later, I opened a law journal and discovered that the same court had reversed itself! It was the first time I could recall a court shifting gears so quickly, and for no apparent reason. I thought they had gotten the message, but apparently it was not mine. Who whispered in their ear?

Recently, I formalized an adoption for the kinship foster aunt of *nine* children. In reviewing the paperwork, I discovered that her subsidy for these children would be $130,000 annually, tax-free, accountability-free, decreasing gradually until the youngest child reached twenty-one. And the money was to be sent to her new home—out of state. These youngsters, you see, had been categorized as "special needs children," and therefore Auntie got a lot more money from foster care.

In this case, the special needs that entitled them to this extra money were the facts that they had been in foster care for five years and they were part of a group of three or more siblings.

The fact that they lived with their aunt for five years and had always lived together with their siblings did not count. They still qualified for the enriched benefits possible under New York state law. None of these children suffered any physical handicap, and it did not seem to matter. My hands were tied. The rate for these children is fixed by statute.

I'm My Own Grandpa

Many of these kinship foster adoptions lead to bizarre configurations. Take the case of three children who stay with their grandmother for four years. They call her Grandma, and this is natural. What is unnatural, however, is a government policy that makes Grandma adopt these children and become their mother. As a result, their biological mother becomes their sister and their aunts and uncles become their siblings! Confused? So am I.

All of this reminds me of the 1950s song: "I'm My Own Grandpa." A recent call from a colleague has convinced me that this has finally happened. It involved a case of two children who had been adopted by their maternal grandmother. Their biological mother, after completing a drug rehabilitation program, wanted weekend and extended holiday visits, but Grandma was resistant. So the mother came to family court and filed a petition seeking visitation rights. She was told by the clerk that only parents, grandparents or siblings could, under New York law, petition the courts for visitation.

The mother, however, was no dummy. Since her parental rights had been terminated, she was no longer a mother. But she told the clerk that since her mother had adopted her own children, she was now their sister—and by law entitled to file the petition. The situation was absurd, but she was right.

Kinship foster care has boomed in New York, driven by the growing number of crack mothers and broken families. It has become a boondoggle of the first magnitude. The program is run by overburdened, often inadequate caseworkers who monitor homes with forms and reports instead of the on-site visits that are so crucial to see if children are thriving from day to day.

Sometimes Blood Is Mud

Following the appearance of an article on foster care that I wrote for the *New York Times,* I received a flood of letters from people, mostly therapists, who chronicled one horror story after another. They told of children brutalized in homes with relatives, supposedly under the supervision of child care workers. One told of a little girl who had been placed with an alcoholic aunt because her mother was a drug addict! Not only was this child deprived of a childhood, and not only were we paying for her mother's crack—but now Auntie could buy a better brand of single-malt scotch.

Meanwhile, the little girl was living in filth.

I learned about two little boys who had been placed with their grandma, also a drunk. She learned too late that her twenty-year-old nephew—another boarder in the home—had been sodomizing the youngsters for months. Then there was the case of the little girl who died of horrible abuse in a kinship foster care home, where she lived with two crackhead aunts. As far as I can tell, their only qualification to take care of her was a thin strand of DNA.

Take the case of Raquel, whose twenty-three-year-old mother was a crack addict. Raquel's mother had four kids in all, and the last two were born addicted to cocaine. Raquel's two aunts had little use for her, but they had plenty of use for the extra $800 that kinship foster care brought into the home every month. This child would die before she reached her fifth birthday, slowly beaten to death by two relatives who got the green light to take care of her. Meanwhile, her mother got pregnant yet again. Not even the death of her daughter deterred her.

Maybe she needed a tougher message. How about a year in jail? At least her new baby would be born drug-free. Or would this violate her "rights"?

Family Preservation Nonsense

Michelle was born in 1990, the third child of a twenty-seven-year-old crack-addicted mother. She was put in a foster care home for two months, and then moved with her two brothers to the kinship foster care home of her aunt, a single welfare mother. Because the assigned caseworker was fired, no one monitored their home for seven months.

In 1991, when someone finally found the file, a caseworker paid an unannounced visit. His findings were appalling: The apartment was a roach-and-fly-infested mess. Dirty clothing was scattered throughout the rooms. The baby was sleeping in a crib with no sheet and was filthy. Did officials remove the children? Not at all. They called a meeting of the "management team."

Indeed, they began "working with" this aunt—family preservation nonsense. On two subsequent visits, however, Auntie was found to be "lethargic" and "incoherent." There were strange and similarly incoherent people who traipsed through the apartment day and night, and the smell of incense wafted in from holes in the wall. There was little food in this loving home, despite the $1,800 a month in public monies pouring in, plus the aunt's own welfare budget.

Terrible, you say. But were the children removed? Not yet. By now, the management team suggested that a "contract" be drawn up with this kinship foster parent, to better outline for her what she must to do to maintain her special status. This lady needed more than a contract. I often wonder to myself, who dreams up such nonsense?

Anyway, four months later, the children were finally removed. They had spent over a year with this creature, who had been masquerading as a caring relative. Why did it take so long? And why were these kids placed there in the beginning?

Lazy bureaucrats and pandering politicians are one answer. What we have been doing with so many social problems—including the shame of foster care—is to simply put a fresh and very expensive bandage on an old, festering wound. We need to clean the infection from the inside out, but that takes courage.

The Operative Word Is Triage

Starting now, judges, caseworkers, politicians and average citizens must pay more attention to the future of these at-risk kids. We must have tough, regular reviews of the children in foster care across this country. When I see a case where a child has been living with a grandmother for four or five years, I immediately ask that she come to court.

If she is providing good care for these children, it is time for the state to bow out. We should recognize her as the new parent, and provide no more costly, endless subsidies. This can be accomplished very quickly, with a simple order of custody or guardianship granted by the court. Neither of these actions costs any money, and both reflect the reality of the home—family is taking care of family.

By doing this, we would be weeding out the imposters and freeing up caseworkers to concentrate on their real cases. Occasionally I encounter a grandmother who boldly asserts that if the kinship foster care money stops, she will no longer take care of the kids. And this gets to the heart of the problem: Is she the kind of grandparent we want raising children?

We are not talking about cutting off Grandma's existing welfare support. If she is entitled to that, she will get it for the children. But why should we give her four times as much as the children would be getting if they were living with their biological parents? Foster care was never intended to be a new strain of permanent, ultra-enriched welfare—or was it?

During a recent adoption conference in my court, a grandmother told me that she would never be relegated to placing her children on public assistance. I asked her what she thought her adoption subsidy was. She did not reply. I pointed out that it was public money with no work requirement. I failed to see the difference, except in the amount.

Now this particular lady was a decent woman. Her daughter was a recovered drug addict who had unfortunately developed a terminal illness. She had three grandchildren, one of them age sixteen, who did not want to be adopted, and if I had approved this woman's adoption petitions, we would have a real mishmash:

Two of the children would become the grandmother's children, rather than her grandchildren. The sister who did not wish to be adopted would remain her granddaughter. Meanwhile, the children's biological mother would become their sister. It would have been a ludicrous situation, the purpose of which was to ensure a continued flow of money. There has to be a better way—and a custody order was my answer.

Goodbye, Grandma—Hello, Foster Parent

In some cases, families living side by side with the exact same number of children receive radically different payments from a diverse menu of entitlements. Take the case of Ms. Jones, who lived in apartment 4-C. Her daughter had become a dysfunctional drug addict, and so the grandmother was raising her four grandchildren. She had applied for and received public assistance checks for the children, receiving about $750 a month for their care, plus food stamps, medical benefits and her own welfare budget.

Two doors down, in apartment 4-E, Ms. Smith had a similar situation. She got a call from child welfare authorities, telling her that her four grandchildren had been removed from their mother's home because her daughter had become an abusive parent. Was she interested in caring for them?

She was told that she would be compensated for their care. Indeed, Ms. Smith was soon receiving $3,000 a month for these four grandchildren, whom the court placed with her. Two doors down, Ms. Jones was hopping mad. How come she had been providing the same care, out of the goodness of her heart, and getting $2,250 a month less than her neighbor, who soon had all sorts of spare cash and new bedroom furniture?

Kinship foster care has also become big business for private, allegedly nonprofit agencies that monitor these homes. Their business is "counseling and monitoring" such homes, and they depend on a steady supply of new participants. They spend a lot of energy educating clients and lobbying politicians on the virtues of kinship foster care. Some groups have even gone so far as to print written instructions on the walls of housing projects throughout the city, advising how to sign up for these benefits.

You simply call the state hotline for child abuse and report that your daughter has taken off for parts unknown, abandoning her children. Caseworkers come out to your house and verify that the children are in your home. The state files its petition in family court, requesting that the children be classified as neglected. Et voilà! You are no longer Grandma, but a kinship foster parent.

It does not matter that Mom may not be so far away after all, and is making regular visits to see her kids. It does not matter that the family is still largely intact. The de facto situation did not change—but the money sure did!

Nonprofit Agencies—the Ultimate Misnomer

The proliferation of these agencies dates back to the explosion of AIDS, crack and homelessness in the 1980s, which left astronomical numbers of children needing stable homes. But it was hard finding traditional foster homes, and so the state hit on the notion of enticing Grandma or Auntie to take care of the kids with a lot of cash incentives. Meanwhile, private agencies that had traditionally located foster parents for the city began to feel threatened. Their work should have ended once relatives opened their doors, but the gravy train was just beginning.

The agencies found new work—at handsome fees—maintaining a "supervisory" role in kinship foster placements, with the city's blessing and your money. Monitoring is certainly important in the early stages of such care, but there is no reason for the city—specifically, its Child Welfare Agency—to pay other groups to do what it should already be doing itself. As a result, public and private groups are covering the same tracks. The overlap is absurd and expensive.

A kinship foster case, for example, is monitored by a private agency caseworker, a supervisor or two, and an agency lawyer, all paid for by taxpayers—as well as a city caseworker, his or her supervisor and a city lawyer, also paid for by taxpayers. That adds up to six people per child. The right hand rarely knows what the left hand is doing; the needs of the children are forgotten. We have kids whose childhoods are slowly disappearing under mounds of paperwork. Private agencies also get a hefty piece of the foster care pie, and the system could run as inefficiently in their absence, or the city's absence. However, many of these groups are well connected.

By now, I can hear the chorus of knee-jerk liberals: What's the big deal, they say? As a result of kinship foster care, poor kids get extra money. Isn't America supposed to be a compassionate country? The problem, I would answer, is that because we have made the scam so attractive, thousands of kids have entered the system who formerly would not—and with so many new kids in foster care around the country, it puts a tremendous strain on the system.

If there were fewer children to be supervised in foster care, the money we saved could be spent to train and retrain the professionals we have. They can make a real difference in the lives of troubled families, and we should give them every chance. As it is, they are just going through the motions, filling out forms, preparing reports and benefiting no one.

Think of the problem as a hospital emergency room: If there are fifty people waiting inside and only two are in critical condition, you might have to wade through forty cases before you reach the people in jeopardy. Where is the triage? It is very much the same with our children; the crises of abuse and neglect should trigger immediate action by highly trained caseworkers. Hours, even minutes, can make a huge difference. But with so many children, by the time you reach the needy ones, often there is nothing to save.

One of the by-products of this overload is the lack of truly qualified caseworkers. To meet growing manpower demands, New York and other jurisdictions have dangerously relaxed the standards by which we hire and train such people. In my view, this creates a real danger for kids.

Many of the caseworkers I see daily are recent immigrants to this country who have marginal academic qualifications, and quite frankly I cannot understand them when they attempt to speak English. If I cannot understand them, how are they supposed to communicate with parents, caregivers and, most important, with children? On two occasions, I said I would only hear the testimony of a child welfare agency worker if they provided me with an interpreter! I could not for the life of me understand how his clients managed to speak with him.

How Do We Fix This Mess?

First, I suggest that when children are placed with relatives, we limit the arrangement to a one-year trial period, during which each home is carefully assessed. Once it is determined that a new family arrangement is working, government involvement—and super-rich subsidies—should end. This would free caseworkers, social workers and administrators to move on and scrutinize the living conditions of children in dangerous homes.

In the long run, we have to ask ourselves the following question: When it comes to family, are we better off today than we were one hundred years ago? How did government get the idea it could intrude into the lives of families who have typically taken care of themselves? We have created a foster care monster, a big business with long tentacles and thousands of patronage jobs. Families have to act responsibly, even if it is uncomfortable. Foster care should be the last resort.

Needless to say, I have been criticized as insensitive for taking on this bureaucracy. But those attacks usually come from people whose livelihoods depend on maintaining this bloated system. If America's foster care programs were creating wonderful, productive children, perhaps all the money we spend would be worth it. Only a fool would complain. But despite the billions, we are in worse shape than ever.

Joyce Had Eleven Children

I will leave you with one story that, to me, says it all.

Joyce had eleven children, and the last four were born addicted to crack cocaine. Her first child was born when she was fourteen. After many costly and futile attempts at family preservation, the city finally brought a neglect case against her and removed all the children from her home. She had three sisters who came to court and reluctantly volunteered to take in the children, instead of placing them with strangers. They were all clearly disgusted with Joyce.

The total cost to taxpayers for this kinship foster care came to $180,000 annually! When the case was finally over, I turned to Joyce and asked why she didn't get some kind of birth control. You have had enough children, I said. At this, her lawyer and the city's lawyer jumped to their feet, looking angry and astounded. Judge, they shouted, you are invading her privacy!

You bet I was. I told them to look around the courtroom, to see the devastation this one woman had caused—to her family, her children and to taxpayers. At this, one sister called out: "Judge, we're her sisters and we wouldn't care if you killed her!" Well, I checked the books, and killing Joyce was not an option.

In the cycle of family dysfunction, Joyce is clearly the starting point. Yet we have legions of academics and bureaucrats who will tell you that society and poverty—in short, all of us—are responsible for creating Joyce.

My answer is, dream on. It is probably too late to salvage the Joyces of this world. Yet we have to start somewhere, to avoid future fiascos. For now, we are stuck with her. The social misery she has created will last well into the next millennium. But we must stop viewing her as a victim.

Let us tell the truth, once and for all: Joyce is a culprit. And if we as a society do not demand that people like her act responsibly, we will continue to get what we have been getting. What is worse, we will deserve it.

CHAPTER 6

Custody Wars Are Battles Without Winners

Modifying Morality: Have We Given Up by Giving In?

Raising kids, even for the most devoted parents, is a crapshoot. You can do everything by the book—from taking your meals and vacations together to being involved in the PTA. Still, you can produce a dysfunctional child.

Conversely, some children who are the products of single, nonfunctioning parents turn out just fine. There must be a DNA strain for surviving childhood. Whatever the formula, giving our children a secure childhood is, at a minimum, their birthright. That is a parent's job.

When I was a child, if you had a classmate who was in therapy, play dates were limited. I guess our parents thought the malady was contagious. At today's slumber parties, kids exchange therapist stories and the latest medication regimens. Children of yesterday's middle class managed to finish college in four years, not five. They baby-sat for pocket money, observed a nightly curfew, and pierced their ears (not their noses and navels).

Back then, girls stopped living at home when they left in a white gown or a pine box. And if guys packed anything, it was cans at the grocery.

How times have changed!

I remember when my older daughter came home with her fiancé from college to get their marriage license. My husband cornered me and said: "They can't sleep together in this house unless they're married." I could see a fight brewing and, as usual, I was in the middle. Quick on my feet, I threw a judicial robe over my jeans, called a neighbor to be a witness, and married the kids on the spot. My husband was happy. The children thought it was amusing.

Today, even my husband, with his Victorian morality, has yielded a bit to conventional mores. Recently he spent an afternoon with our youngest daughter, Nicole, and her significant other, who were looking for an apartment together. That was a big step forward, yet he is still in significant denial.

He will not call her at her boyfriend's apartment. He wonders whether she has begun menstruating (she's twenty-seven) and he still buys her oversized stuffed animals for her birthday. These are funny stories, but they are also examples of give-and-take in a home where parents are involved and care deeply about their kids.

Our Legal System Fuels the Fire

Not all children are so lucky. Divorce has reached epidemic proportions in our culture, with almost half of our children enduring their parents' acrimonious parting of the ways. And while not all problems can be traced to such ruptures, it surely is a factor in long-term child development.

Unfortunately, our courts promote these wars, instead of easing transitions for children. And battles over child custody are at the heart of this contradiction. Children are the ultimate victims of these custody battles, and in this chapter I hope to expose some legal inequities that have ravaged too many families. If we truly believe that men and women are created equal—as parents as well as individuals—it is time our courts reflected this.

Some may be outraged at my call for joint custody laws, but after you finish reading some of the case histories that follow, I think you will agree with me that this reform is long overdue.

Most important, it is time for bickering spouses to stop treating our courts like a playpen. If you clog up a court docket with frivolous and selfish arguments—like false allegations of child sex abuse—we can and should make you pay. If you want to throw mud, do it in your own backyard.

Fathers Are Parents, Too

Our priorities are in disarray, starting with the way we talk about child custody. While the United States legal system is allegedly gender-neutral, we say that a mother "lost custody" of children if they wind up living with their father. We would never say that about the father. They are—after all the hogwash about fairness—*supposed* to lose custody. We have made them into second-class parents, and then wonder why they do not always behave appropriately.

Take the case of Melissa, who was eight. Her parents, both in their thirties, handsome and educated, were ushered into my court. The issue was visitation: Dad wanted three weekends a month, but Mom was only willing to give him alternate weekends. Not the issue of the decade, but these folks and their lawyers were prepared to embark on a weeklong trial of mudslinging and turn this into the second Scopes trial, complete with mental health evaluations and home studies. They did not seem to care about the impact on their child.

I explained that what Dad wanted was six days of visitation a month, which was not at all unreasonable. The angry mother responded that she was a working woman, and was at a loss to understand how I could deprive her of three consecutive weekends with her child. An understandable concern, but parents must realize that when they divorce, *all* the rules change. The only constant is that children must be secure in the belief that they still have two parents. Four days of visitation a month for Dad does not do it—and neither does six.

Men Had the Money and Women Used the Kids

It all comes down to money and power. For decades, men held the purse strings in United States divorce proceedings. The rules changed when women's advocates helped spark a legal revolution, installing the doctrine of equitable distribution of property. But women continue to hold the emotional vise: the kids. They have become the central pawns in divorce proceedings.

If Dad did not pay last week's child support on time, Mom arbitrarily cuts off visitation. If Dad has a new girlfriend, Mom decides that she will not allow the kids to sleep at his house. If Dad wants relief, he has to come to court.

When this happens, I ask Mom: Who monitors your bedroom? She almost always answers that she would do *nothing* to offend her child. But why, I respond, should she assume any less of the father? It is a question of simple fairness.

In my years on the bench, I have resolved thousands of custody and visitation disputes. I have never had a case where one parent was perfect and the other was a beast. I have had a fair sampling, however, where both were beasts. As my grandmother used to say, every pot has a cover.

Beauty Fades, Dumb Is Forever

When I began working in family court, one of my first cases dealt with a battle over child support paid to a middle-class woman and her three children. Her ex-husband was a lawyer, and they hated each other like poison. She demonized him to the children. He, in turn, refused to give her a penny.

Sylvia was in court at least once a month, and after several years of this, I told her: "You're wasting your life with this vendetta. He's a rat, but it's your life that's ebbing away." Twenty-two years later, they are *still* in court.

This lawyer has been jailed six times for contempt of court orders. He had no life, Sylvia had no life and their children were the casualties of war. They hate their deadbeat father, and they have endured a neurotic, obsessive mother. They spent their childhood in a war zone. What is the point?

It always amazes me that the same parents who would tear the heart out of a stranger trying to harm their kids would embark on divorce campaigns that destroy these same children. And the worst thing is that both parents will typically insist they are doing this in the kids' "best interests."

Consider the billions spent in resolving custody cases and their wrenching aftermath: Life savings are squandered on lawyers' fees, adding up to decades of debt. Court time taken up with these go-rounds is prohibitively expensive. Money is spent on therapists for the parents, and therapists for the children. Special education is needed for those emotionally battered kids of divorce who cannot function in regular classrooms. Millions are spent on legal experts who testify to the venality of one parent or the other. We pay a huge price for all of this, in emotional and fiscal terms, and there is no end in sight.

The Solution: Joint Custody

In resolving matrimonial property cases, our legal system is guided by the rule of equitable distribution. This means that separating families have to share their wealth equally. If a court ever deviates from that standard, there has to be a very good reason. It is a good rule, but we seem to have forgotten the children. They have a right to be nurtured equally by both parents, and it is time for our legal system to respect this in fact, not just in concept. I propose that we create a new presumption of joint custody in divorce cases. Unless there is a valid reason, joint parenting would be the rule rather than the exception.

Under this new rule, *both* parents would continue to have responsibility for their children. Such co-parenting does not necessarily mean that Mom and Dad would put in the same hours, but it would mean that fathers could no longer be relegated to the status of intermittent, weekend parents. Under such a rule, we would end the selfish assumption that divorce is mainly a battle between two adults. At long last, we would be putting children's interests first.

Beyond its inherent fairness, we might expect other benefits from a joint custody rule. A recent report released by the census bureau revealed that 25 percent of noncustodial parents made child support payments. However, among the parents who have joint custody or visitation, 79 percent paid some or all of the support due. Consider the problem of welfare dependency and divorce. We have long heard the complaint that a lack of day care keeps women on the dole. This might become a nonissue, since parents who are not together could get jobs and work different shifts, ensuring that children would not be neglected. We would be sending a message that divorce does not end your responsibility to support a family.

We would also ensure even-handed treatment for

fathers. In most jurisdictions, fathers are on equal legal footing with mothers on all issues involving the family. Courts are supposed to approach cases of child custody, support payments or visitation rights in what we call a gender-neutral posture. It sounds fair, and it is fair. But it is a myth. Judges are not enforcing these gender laws fairly, and few seem to care.

Wake Up, Dad

American fathers are led down a primrose path every day in our family courts, often with disastrous legal results. They wind up in the Land of Gender Bias, where they are systematically stripped of their rights, often without the slightest idea of why it is happening to them.

Take the case of Susan. She was married to Eric and they had a beautiful baby boy, Casey. Both were employed, earning roughly comparable salaries. When they divorced, Eric was ordered to pay Susan $100 per week in child support. Before long, both found new mates. Eric had another child with his new wife, and Susan had a new child with her second husband. But then Susan decided to stay at home with the new baby and quit her job. She came to family court seeking additional child support money from Eric, who was outraged.

Indeed, he had faithfully paid his child support and had been responsible in his budget, which allowed him

to have another child. Why should he be further bur-
dened by a lifestyle decision that Susan made on her
own? The court, however, sided with the mother. It was
all right for Susan to quit her job, become a full-time
mom and seek more child support payments from her
ex-husband. After all, motherhood is motherhood. But
what if Eric had chosen to make the same decision—to
stay at home with his new baby? Very likely, he would
have been called a bum and a deadbeat. The sheriff
would have been on his case in a minute.

If You Behave, We'll Only Take One of Your Kids

Then there is the case of Gregory, who had three children. All were removed from the mother's custody
after she was found guilty of neglect. Sometime later,
she died of a drug overdose. Meanwhile, Gregory was
serving a one-to-four-year sentence for car theft. But
he kept in regular contact with his two older children,
who were in the same foster home with their one-
year-old sister. When Gregory was released, he got a
job, found a suitable apartment, completed the parenting program that the state had demanded and regularly visited his kids. He was one of the few who had
turned his life around.

Soon, the children's caseworker faced a knotty
problem: The foster mother was willing to return the
two older children to their father, but not the baby.

The caseworker approved this plan and told Gregory that if he agreed to give up custody of the youngest, she would recommend that the other kids be returned to him. Needless to say, Gregory protested this deal. When he "outrageously" demanded the return of all three of his children, according to the caseworker's report, she called his parole officer and suggested that he was being "uncooperative." Perhaps a parole review was in order, she said.

Gregory's tail was now neatly tucked between his legs and he agreed to this devil's bargain. He had no choice whatsoever—until the case came to me.

Rest assured, after a grueling hour in the witness stand, this dictatorial caseworker was reduced to rubble. Dad got all three of his children back, and they are thriving today, six years later. In another courtroom the deal might have slipped through without notice. But I am on the lookout for gender bias and I have no patience with it. I was relieved that Gregory got a measure of justice, but I ask you: Would a caseworker have pulled this stunt on a mother?

Equal Rights for Men—Until They Seek Custody

For the past twenty years, we have encouraged men to become involved with their children, from conception and Lamaze through birthing, feeding, diapering and quality time. We have fooled them into believing that the law means what it says, when it promises that fathers and mothers are treated equally in our courts.

When men seek custody of their children, courts make them jump through hoops. Moms get the red carpet treatment. That is the lesson Tim learned. He was a twenty-four-year-old auto mechanic, a nice kid with very bad judgment when it came to choosing a mate.

Robin, twenty-six, had two children before she met Tim. She also had a drug problem. When their child was born with cocaine in her system, the city stepped in and removed all three kids from Robin's care. Tim, who had separated from Robin, went running to the Child Welfare Agency, demanding his daughter. He was living at home with his mother, his father and his brother, all of whom were employed. Here is what he had to do, according to the city:

First, he had to establish paternity, proving that he was the biological father of his child. Tim did this. Next, the caseworker told him that before he could even be considered for custody, he had to take parenting classes. He had to provide the name of the person who would be caring for his child while he worked during the day. He had to establish a permanent, independent residence. There was not a scintilla of evidence that he was an unfit parent, but these were the rules that Tim had to follow. He met all of the conditions.

Meanwhile, Robin the drug addict had it easy. All she had to do was enroll herself in a drug treatment program and get on welfare. That, my friends, was it.

These deals go down every day. When I asked the caseworker about the gender disparity here, her answer was simple: "Well, she's the mother." Ultimately, Tim won custody of his daughter. Robin's mother took the other two kids, and Robin went on to have two more addicted babies. But not with Tim.

When are we going to enforce our gender bias laws without bias? If you think the mother-father disparity is outrageous, consider the sexual abuse syndrome, and how it affects visitation and custody disputes. Here, the judicial impotence—and chronic blindness to men's rights—would appall you.

The Ultimate Weapon: He Abused the Kids

For too long, child sex abuse went undetected, under-reported and underprosecuted in our legal system. Too many children were destroyed by the abuse of parents, caregivers or strangers, and it has only been in the last decade that America took a tougher line on this unspeakable crime.

Having said this, however, the legal system has also been guilty of overreaction. At times, it seems to be restaging the Salem witch trials.

Sexual abuse of children must be deplored at every level, but social agencies and judges should be as vigilant in exposing false claims as they are in prosecuting deviant dads. In recent years, mothers have come into court alleging that their mates have sexually abused their children. It makes the system cower in fear, and the first reaction is usually to cut off a father's visitation rights, "just to be on the safe side." Needless to say, this can make ugly domestic disputes even more explosive.

Take the case of Joseph, an educated, middle-class guy who found himself on the wrong end of a paternity suit. He had a brief, two-time affair with Sally, a single woman in her forties, who became pregnant and decided to have a child. After the liaison, they had no contact for years. She never told him she had a baby. The child was two and one-half years old before Sally initiated a case in family court to have Joseph declared the father. He was, in fact, the second or third possibility since her previous cases were dismissed, when blood tests excluded her other boyfriends. Other than the child support she demanded, Sally was unequivocally resistant to building any relationship between father and daughter.

Once the blood tests identified Joseph as the father, however, he immediately volunteered to pay support. He also requested visitation with his daughter. Sally reluctantly agreed to visits, but only under her direct supervision. I accommodated her, but only to ease the transition to a time when Dad and his daughter could have unsupervised visits, where both could get to know each other better.

Just before the unsupervised visits were scheduled to start, Sally made a flurry of accusations against

Joseph, accusing him of abusive conduct. A full investigation by child welfare caseworkers found no evidence of inappropriate behavior. Hearing after hearing on the matter revealed only a nice guy trying to visit with his daughter and build a solid relationship.

Finally, in desperation, Sally alleged that Joseph had sexually abused their daughter. Now, Joseph's name would be in the social service system's computer forever. He was interviewed by a cadre of caseworkers and police. The child was subjected to both internal physical examinations and endless hours of therapy— all finding no evidence of abuse. Still, Sally persisted in making these allegations. The situation was rapidly getting out of control.

Ultimately, after an extensive trial, I awarded Joseph full-time custody of his daughter and Sally only supervised time, after she persisted in allegations of abuse during her unsupervised visits. I concluded that her persistent cries of sex abuse were only the tip of the iceberg of her mental instability, and that it was inappropriate for her to raise the child by herself. The daughter—at last report—is thriving in her father's care.

The case of Sally and Joseph is by no means unique. I suspect that the pattern has become distressingly familiar in other family courtrooms as well.

Once, a mother complained to me that her ex-husband slept in the bed with his three-year-old daughter during their visits. She wanted his visitation rights sharply curtailed. I looked disapprovingly at the father, who conceded this had happened, although he insisted that he had tried to coax the girl to sleep in her own room. The mother's attorney believed the case was won at this point and, quite frankly, so did I. This was highly inappropriate behavior.

Then I asked the mother where the child slept when she was with her. "Why, with me," she answered. "She's always slept with us."

Stupid but true. When the couple separated, the daughter continued to sleep with her mother. But Mom set new rules for Dad. When at his house, the daughter had to sleep alone. It was a cunning way of manipulating the child and her father.

Over the last decade, I have had perhaps thirty or more such allegations come before me. But less than 10 percent have had any validity, because more often than not mothers are simply trying to punish men. And they are supported in this by a dubious industry comprised of thinly credentialed, so-called experts.

My first experience with one of these "experts" was an art therapist, and it was as frightening as it was telling. She produced a picture drawn by a four-year-old girl whose mother insisted that the girl was being sexually fondled during visitation with her father. The drawing depicted a school bus, with a driver in the front seat and a child in the back of the bus. "Clearly," she reasoned, "the positioning of the driver so far from the child leaves little doubt that this child has been the victim of abuse." This kind of voodoo passes for science, and it is preposterous.

I recently went to a series of seminars on child abuse. No lecturer, no expert offered any insight on how to spot false allegations of abuse. There were lots of hints on how to uncover sex abuse, from bed-wetting to doll therapy to music and art play, all the amorphous theories by self-styled advocates. But no one talked about how false allegations can ruin fathers and their children. A child wrongfully denied the love of a father is as much a travesty as a child forced to endure such abuse.

Even if trial judges have the courage to question allegations of sexual abuse, fathers are doomed if they push the issue in appellate courts. Those judges almost invariably play it safe, cutting off children from their fathers as a matter of course. It can take months to investigate such matters, and all the while we have deprived kids of the fundamental right to see their dads.

I have given custody of children to fathers in most of the cases where mothers persist in making unfounded allegations of sexual abuse. If these women are prepared to torment their children and lie to the court simply to get control in a long-running family dispute, I consider them unfit to parent.

We will see more of these problems until fathers organize to demand fairer treatment. So get it together, dads: You have a legitimate legal beef and you need to make this a public issue. Right now, the courts do not hear you.

The New Nuclear Family

My experience with the nuclear family is both personal and professional. When my husband and I married, I had two young children and he had three. The five kids have grown into adults, loving each other, their parents and stepparents. It was not always easy. Splitting holidays, birthdays and special occasions were hard on all of us. Much of what we did was trial and error. Our union and our children's success is a testament to hard work—and a lot of luck.

Children thrive on love, attention and affection. Today's nuclear families are often a mixture of stepparents, half-siblings and stepgrandparents. These amalgams can produce wonderful, nurturing homes, because children love and depend on the adults who take care of them, no matter who they are.

Why, then, does our legal system often require us to terminate the rights of these nurturers unless there is a biological relationship? It makes no sense, especially to the children we are supposed to be protecting.

When Lisa married Carl, she was twenty-two and had two-year-old Alex from a brief prior relationship. They had two children together, and Carl was a wonderful father to all three kids. But after nine years of marriage, Lisa became involved with her decorator, and the couple separated. Carl wanted only to continue to be an involved father with his three children—but Lisa would not allow him to visit Alex unless he capitulated to what were unreasonable financial demands.

He was out of luck, because in New York the law gave him no right to contact and visitation with the child whom he had raised and loved. Never mind that Alex might need attention from both of her parents; we have a system that respects biological ties and little else. Lisa was adamant and Carl was stymied, but I quickly pointed out a quirk in the law: Anyone can seek legal custody of a child, as long as they prove that a biological parent is unfit.

Turning to Lisa's lawyer, I agreed that she had him over a legal barrel on the visitation issue. But I also pointed out that her position was hurtful to Alex. Accordingly, I was prepared to find her unfit as a parent and award Carl full custody of all three children. You should have seen Lisa's jaw drop! Her capitulation was swift and complete, and we settled the case without a trial. Today, Carl visits all three of his children, and he supports them reasonably and fairly. As for Lisa, she learned an important lesson.

If You Waste the Court's Time, It Will Cost You

I wish other parents could get the same message. Maybe then they would think twice before clogging our court system with selfish custody battles. Of the three branches of government, the judiciary is the only direct service provider. That is, citizens actually use its services to resolve disputes. Most people who divorce resolve their differences with a minimal drain on the courts, yet others involve themselves in protracted litigation that wastes time and costs taxpayers millions of dollars.

Let us get tough with this latter group. I propose they should be required to undergo mandatory mediation before they are allowed to launch a long and expensive legal battle. Some states are beginning to adopt similar rules, and they should apply nationwide. While not every divorcing couple needs such governmental intervention, a great many would benefit from learning—in advance—how much an interminable custody battle would affect their children, not to mention their pocketbook. We would settle a lot more cases before trial.

Get real, Mom and Dad: If you cannot act reasonably and responsibly as parents in resolving custody disputes, you will pay a price. If you want to gobble up court time with a nasty, self-serving battle, be prepared to sit through a six-week mediation course first, at your own expense, of course.

You just might learn something.

CHAPTER 7

System Scammers

I Learned It at My Mother's Knee

The phone rings, and your eight-year-old son answers. "Hi, Aunt Bee!" he says. You quickly whisper, "Tell her I'm in the shower." The lesson: Grownups lie and it is OK. The seeds are sown, and scams begin.

For most children of our social system, the lies usually have economic repercussions. Grandma tells Mom to leave the house for a while, because the social worker is coming in the morning. According to the rules of kinship foster care eligibility, she is not supposed to be living with you. So Grandma warns you not to tell the social worker that you saw Mom an hour or so ago.

Your dad comes by every Saturday and slips your

mom $100 in cash. Mom tells the welfare people she does not know where he is, or even who he is. Stories like these are all too familiar, but the message to kids is always the same.

A fourteen-year-old begins selling drugs. He lives with both his parents. His father gets disability benefits, but works off the books for a moving company. He has never paid taxes. The son sees no difference between himself and the dishonesty of his father.

Mom trades her food stamps for drugs, and the kids are forced to beg from neighbors for food. A toddler is beaten because he is not toilet-training fast enough. The welts become infected, and he listens as Mom tells the emergency room doctor, "He fell while playing."

Lying is learned at Mother's knee.

The lying I reveal in this chapter has a common thread—money. It's about people using the art of the lie or the scam to cheat and pocket taxpayer dollars to which they are not legitimately entitled. When society creates well-intentioned social programs to aid the truly needy, the scammers are ready to find the loophole and get in on the financial action.

If you can come up with a good enough scheme and package it in politically correct lingo, you can usually sell it. The cheaters must be exposed, not only because they take our money, but because this insidious national pastime has made Americans suspicious of one another.

If You Come Up with a Good Enough Lie, You Can Get Over on the Government

Scams permeate the system from top to bottom. They range from individual cases of fraud and abuse to multimillion-dollar rip-offs by so-called nonprofit agencies, all in the name of helping disadvantaged people. Either way, scams contribute to a prevailing lack of ethics in our society; they build dishonesty into the foundations of our social service programs.

Individuals who rip off the system are occasionally caught and sometimes even punished. Lowering the boom on large agencies is a real challenge. They have the veneer of respectability, even though they plunder the public purse with no less abandon. They are far more dangerous because of their clout and big-name supporters, and it can be suicidal to question their integrity.

If we ever hope to purge ourselves of these scams, we must come clean and tell the truth about the cheaters in our midst.

When individuals cheat, not only are their children nurtured in an atmosphere of family dishonesty, but the needy, honest folks for whom the entitlements were designed become suspect. Today's welfare reform movement has been inspired at least in part by the program's abusers. So everybody suffers.

The Middle Class Gets In on the Action

These days, there is a new breed of custody case wangling its way through our family courts. The object of these cases is not to provide a child with a more nurturing environment, but to provide the family with more of your money. Great-grandma is in her eighties, and the thirty-something parents of her four-year-old great-grandson want to relinquish custody to her. Why would they do such a thing? I listened to their cock-and-bull story about wanting Grandma "to have a new sense of purpose" in her life. Of course, these parents still intend to see their young son on weekends, when they are not working.

I tell these folks that I am not as dumb as I look, and unless I get the real story I intend to unleash child welfare workers on the family. Finally the truth comes out: It seems these middle-class parents, who earn sixty thousand dollars annually, want Grandma to have custody so she can get public assistance. This, in turn, will qualify her for free day care. The parents' income precludes such a freebie, and paying for day care, they say, would be "a hardship."

Right. The same "hardship" that millions of other hardworking families somehow manage to endure. I quickly dismissed Grandma's petition, but I am sure we have not heard the end of this conniving family. They will probably look for a more sympathetic listener who does not ask too many embarrassing questions.

Some children are voluntarily placed in foster care by their parents, and since the law requires that relatives be explored first as foster parents, they wind up with Grandma. The kid who is getting $200 per month from welfare now gets $600 per month from foster care.

Some parents voluntarily surrender all of their parental rights and consent to the adoption of their kids by a relative. The adoption subsidy, three or four times the amount of welfare, ensures this family a permanent income, thanks to you, for twenty-one years. And the reality of the family is unchanged.

The practical implications of these scams have tentacles that transcend the individual case. In New York City, there is a backlog of six thousand adoptions. At least half of that number are legitimate. The legitimate ones must wait for years while we wade through these intrafamilial scams that do not change the family one iota. But the powerfully connected agencies that make big bucks ministering to these adoptions have a vested interest in maintaining this judicially approved social fiasco. And woe to the judges who expose them.

A Condo in Atlantic City—and You Paid

By now, most of us have heard endless stories about lower-income people trying to scam the system. But middle-class folks are no less innovative when it comes to milking the taxpayers. After all, they figure, since they help pay for these programs, they deserve a free ride, too. What is the harm if one more family climbs aboard the gravy train? The harm, of course, is that every time somebody cheats the system, no matter how rich or poor, we *all* lose.

While I am repelled by scamming, I must salute the ingenuity of those who have mastered the art. Once, in the midst of a rape trial, the grandmother of the accused fifteen-year-old assailant was called to testify. She told me that her grandson was not in New York City on the date in question—and she could prove it.

She quickly fished out her Gold MasterCard, along with a statement showing a flurry of purchases in New Jersey on the day of the attack. The boy, she insisted, was shopping with her in Atlantic City.

I examined the bill, totaling $970 in purchases for the month, including some hefty restaurant charges. I grew very curious about what this lady did for a living, because I was once turned down for a gold card, even though I was a veteran lawyer. Over the objections of the boy's lawyer, I asked the woman—and her response bowled me over. She was a kinship foster parent for some of her nieces and nephews, she said, and got $3,100 a month from the state, in addition to her own public assistance check.

She was down at the Jersey shore, by the way, on the semiannual jaunt she takes to her time-share condo in Atlantic City. The kids *love* it there, she confided.

Ask and Ye Shall Discover

One of the lessons I have learned is that there are two kinds of judging. Some liken their job to that of an umpire; they sift through information that lawyers provide. Then they make decisions based on that information. I am generally unhappy with that approach, unless the lawyering is superb, because without quality information you can make mistakes.

In life, as on the bench, you are either passive or active. I prefer the second kind of judging—where the court actively seeks the truth. I ask a lot of questions. The decisions judges are called upon to render are far too important to rely on less than all the facts. When juries are involved, the role of a trial judge is limited. But bench trials, especially in family court, allow a judge far more latitude.

Those jurists who read this book and say they have never encountered the problems I discuss are kidding themselves. I see a steady stream of scammers every day, from all walks of life, and it is just not possible for them all to be filtering into my courtroom.

Scams in the Name of Charity, or If You're Going to Steal, Steal Big

Sometimes scams benefit social service agencies, which are supposed to be reuniting families, not keeping them apart. Take the case of a woman who needed a new apartment in order to remove her kids from foster care. They had been temporarily placed there after her prior home had burned down. The bill to taxpayers for foster care was $80,000 a year. After months of looking for a new home, the woman found a suitable apartment for $679 a month.

But there was a bureaucratic catch: The city would only allot $612 for the apartment, so the kids continued to stay in foster care. The city saved a whopping $67 per month, while the state continued to dish out $80,000. A family remained broken, and taxpayers were still paying through the nose. But think of the private agencies who made out like bandits for their "services rendered" in foster care. For them, this catch-22 was a gold mine.

It is a common pattern. When you are dealing with large charitable organizations, a scam is hard to detect, especially if dubious programs are cloaked in phrases like "helping the handicapped." Only by looking closer do you realize that compassion is big business—often at public expense.

State and local governments, for example, are under federal regulations to provide therapeutic intervention for handicapped infants up to three years old. This is a great idea if properly administered, because it can give these children an important head start. The problem, however, is that these programs can be easily abused. Special schools are set up for handicapped children, and they feature all-encompassing programs, including speech therapy (ST), occupational therapy (OT), physical therapy (PT), social work (SW) and educational therapy (ET).

Not all kids need such services, but the costs at "center-based" programs are the same for all children. If a child needs speech therapy, he gets ST, OT, PT, SW and ET. We treat these centers like sacred cows. No one would dream of challenging them—until you take a closer look at the bill.

Does Freddy Need Your $38,000 to Sing Songs?

A bright, engaging three-year-old, Freddy, had a mild orthopedic problem, and he was enrolled in a special school set up by a well-known charity. A baby when he began the program, Freddy was also in foster care. He seemed to be doing well, and I was encouraged by his progress when I reviewed a petition seeking to keep him in the special school. Then one of his teachers made a passing comment that simply defied common sense.

She was attempting to justify the need for social therapy in addition to Freddy's physical therapy, testifying that at nine months, he should be reluctant to go from one adult to another. Since he showed no reluctance when separated from his foster mother, the teacher said, he needed therapy.

I began wondering, what else does Freddy need?

As the case progressed, I watched a videotape of a typical day at the special school. It looked remarkably similar to any nursery school, only the parents were there with the kids. The children played on little mats, the moms talked and occasionally a therapist entered the room and showed a mother how to position her baby. The highlight of the tape came when Freddy and the other children sat in a circle and sang songs, just like any other kids.

The cost for each student in this special school was $38,000 a year.

I began asking a stream of questions: If Freddy needed a physical therapist, why not simply send one to his home three times a week? I was told that a "team approach" was best, since it gave parents the chance to interact. But why, I asked myself, did we need such an expensive setting? When one of my kids needed speech therapy, I simply hired a speech therapist. If I wanted to socialize with moms whose kids had a speech problem, I could do it on my own time. All of a sudden, this program began to look like a scam. The administrators did not care about taxpayers; they had set up an elaborate cost structure and then fit kids into the program, not the other way around.

How, you might ask, did I get involved in this issue? The initial exposure was innocent enough. For years, family court judges were required to approve petitions that referred kids to these special schools. The city usually consented to such requests, with no questions asked. In 1993, however, the city and state decided to remove these cases from family court and designated an administrative agency to oversee them. The cutoff date for referrals was July 1, 1993, and in June of that year there was an explosion: Family courts were inundated with thousands of last-minute petitions by these schools.

Why the rush, I thought? Why were they so afraid to go through a new administrative route? Curious, I picked six of these petitions at random and began my own investigation. Something seemed definitely out of line.

I called the schools, identified myself and asked for the attendance records of these six handicapped children. Two had never attended the program. One attended two days and the school was billing for an entire summer session, approximately $3,600. Three went twice a week for two and a half hours a day, and the schools were billing taxpayers for a regular five-day program. I was dumbfounded.

It Was Like Finding Out That Mother Teresa Was Running a Bawdy House

Talk about a betrayal of public trust! Digging deeper, I learned that these schools had been padding their expenses for years by billing us for unnecessary therapy sessions, double-billing Medicaid, billing for children who scarcely attended and routinely falsifying documents. In family court, we sounded a wake-up call and put program officials on notice that the courts were on to their game. But not before hundreds of millions of dollars had been wasted. And ultimately, who was going to crack the whip? The city was in the midst of an election, and the last thing the incumbent wanted was to see a bunch of parents and little handicapped kids picketing on the City Hall steps.

Sometimes the scams feed on each other. Consider the following, not-uncommon scenario: A foster parent has two children. The rate she receives for each child is increased dramatically if the child is classified as handicapped. The definition of handicapped is quite broad, and encompasses everything from profound physical to emotional conditions. So foster Mom tells her social worker that Jenny and Sue are hyperactive. The private agency doctor sees the kids for about a half hour, listens to their symptoms as recounted by foster Mom and recommends a special therapeutic nursery school. Jenny and Sue are enrolled in one of these pricey schools, where they get ST, OT, PT, SW and ET. Foster Mom gets an additional $600 a month; everybody is happy except the taxpayers, who do not even know they have been fleeced.

It Wasn't VD, It Was Diaper Rash

We had better luck exposing a rip-off that surfaced in the early 1980s, when I was in Bronx Family Court.

We began to be deluged with sex abuse cases involving toddlers; the sole allegation in each petition was that the child tested positive for chlamydia, a sexually transmitted disease.

The medical findings were based on lab tests, which doctors requested after routine examinations of children. If a court concluded that an infant or toddler had chlamydia, it could rule that the child had been abused—either by a parent, or by a parent who was neglectful in failing to protect the child.

I wondered to myself if a whole new generation of sex perverts had come out of nowhere, because the men coming before me as defendants looked pretty reasonable, and they were stunned to be facing such accusations. They strongly denied having abused their babies, and I realized it was time for me to start asking questions: We were faced with the prospect of removing children from their families. We were going to be branding their fathers as sexual molesters wholesale, a label that would remain with them forever. We had to be careful.

Now, most of us want to believe that hospitals and laboratories do not make mistakes. For months, judges in New York were making findings of sexual abuse based on these chlamydia test results. Amid this epidemic, I began conducting a trial involving a two-year-old girl who had tested positive. She came from an intact home and the parents seemed to be lovely, responsible people. The lawyering in this case, however, was inept at best. I demanded that the family's lawyers produce a doctor from the hospital where the test had been conducted. I wanted to question him about the disease and the testing process itself. What I learned was remarkable.

The doctor told me there are two types of tests generally utilized to detect chlamydia. The first, a nonspecific test for infection, took only one day to yield results. Its findings were general, however, and not specific enough to support a finding of sexual abuse. What seemed like chlamydia could also be a rash or other infection. The second, more specific, test took five days to complete. Only with the second test could a court reliably make a finding of sexual abuse. The first test cost $10; the second cost $150.

In the trial before me, the child had been tested on June 1, yet the laboratory had reported her positive for chlamydia on June 2, billing the city $150. That was clearly impossible, based on the doctor's testimony. I promptly reviewed similar test results in other cases and found the same chronological discrepancy. There was no way a laboratory could have tested a child on day one and reported a definitive finding on day two.

No way, of course, unless they were running a scam. If you do not know how to ask the right questions, who would know that a $150 billing to the city should, in fact, be only $10? Our great sex abuse scare was driven by dollars and cents. The laboratories had acted unethically. They had bilked both insurance and

Medicaid. We in the courts, relying on their findings, had destroyed families. Once this game was uncovered, the practice was quickly halted. I have not seen a chlamydia case in years.

But the damage was done. How many parents were traumatized by this tawdry rip-off? Where could they go to get back their dignity and self-respect?

Is It a 20 Percent Success or an 80 Percent Flop?

In the late 1980s and 1990s, lots of people were trying to get money for programs known as "Alternatives to Incarceration." The idea was that we could save the public a fortune by not putting criminals in jail. Instead, we would treat them with special community programs at a lesser cost.

Liberal politicians and their community allies lauded this approach as an enlightened response to overcrowded jails. It was, they said, a great step forward for criminal rehabilitation. But the results tell a different story.

Whenever an attorney for a juvenile comes before me and requests that his or her client be sent to one of these "alternative" ventures, I always insist that the program director appear in court. With few exceptions, the scenario is distressingly similar: These programs will take just about anybody. They justify their continued existence with statistics indicating that they are "successful" with anywhere from 10 to 25 percent of their clients.

Indeed, say these program directors, we save the taxpayers hundreds of thousands of dollars in jail costs. It all sounds terrific until you start asking some questions. A 25 percent success rate is fine, I'll say, but what about the other 75 percent who returned to a life of crime? What are the costs to the victims of these people, the costs to the community at large?

The answer, obviously, is that we were kidding ourselves. If these programs do not get tough and weed out the truly hardened offenders, we ought to give these "service providers" the boot and put them out of business. Keeping them on the public payroll puts the public at risk. When it comes to violent criminals, a 25 percent success rate is one we can all live without.

Political and Racial Racketeers: Where Is Your Constituency?

One of the depressing realities of our society is that a few ideologues with loud voices seem to have disproportionate influence over our lives. They accomplish this with intimidation. If you have the audacity to disagree with them publicly, there is no reasoned debate. They give you a label and you are supposed to capitulate, or tuck your tail between your legs and fade away.

Being a bully is one of the oldest—and most effective—scams around. You can rob people blind, until they realize that you are full of baloney.

When I first began to question some of the problems I described earlier with kinship foster care, it marked the first time that any New York judge had questioned the wisdom of this program. The costs were getting out of hand, I said, and the fraud being perpetrated on the public was unacceptable. We had to take back control. I made these comments during a public forum on the issue which was convened by the Bar Association of the City of New York. There were eight people on an evening panel—seven advocates of the program, and me.

The magnificent seven told inspirational stories about how kinship foster care was serving the poor. The packed audience applauded, but then I gave a different view. While laudable in design, I said, the program was becoming a big business that sanctioned outright fraud in the name of foster care. If the object is to increase the flow of funds to the poor, be honest and say so. If the goal is to enhance welfare payments, be honest and say so. But do not fool the public by giving welfare just another name.

I told several stories to illustrate my point, relating cases where kinship foster parents as well as the agencies that allegedly supervised them were not only robbing the system, but failing to protect children. By the end of the evening, I believe that I opened many people's eyes to widespread abuse.

Then the pontiffs of political correctitude got busy.

I learned that the head of one of these foster care agencies had written an indignant letter to the Commission on the Judiciary demanding my immediate removal from the bench. She claimed that anyone who could recount such stories was obviously insensitive to poor people and thus should not be serving in family court. It made no difference that the stories were true. I got a copy of her letter, and while it was not the usual protocol to respond personally, I felt compelled to vent my outrage. The sole purpose of my appearance on the panel was to show the other side of the issue. Everyone knew that was why I had been invited in the first place. Whatever happened to free speech, and how dull a one-sided debate!

The key issue was fairness. It was clearly one thing for these people to hold a love fest and preach their knee-jerk drivel to the converted. But God forbid someone should get up in a public meeting and disagree.

In one sense, it was no surprise. Those with a financial and political investment in the status quo get uncomfortable when someone questions their wisdom. Yet I am quite comfortable questioning people who spend my tax dollars to support themselves. The long and short of it is that her call for my termination was rejected, and I am still here.

Unfortunately, the desire to stifle free speech is still very much with us. Racketeers who rake in public money do not tolerate anyone challenging them, and they will use any trick to keep us quiet. Guilt is a classic weapon: They have no shame in trying to make us feel collectively responsible for crime, teen pregnancy, welfare, homelessness and the breakdown of social order. If they had their way, we would feel responsible for bad weather, too.

So wake up, folks. Criminals are responsible for crime. Rip-off artists who masquerade as social service providers should also be held accountable. Let us not waste any more time or public money on an endless game of three-card monte.

It is a game we will always lose.

CHAPTER 8

Get Real, Get Responsible, or: I'm a Victim, I'm a Victim, I'm a Victim

Whose Trash Is It Anyway?

One of my closest friends is a dear man named Marvin. Many years ago he inherited an apartment building in Brooklyn. The building had a large courtyard, and Marvin was soon cited by the city for allowing huge amounts of garbage to accumulate in the yard. He immediately arranged to have the trash removed, at substantial expense. But month after month, the citations arrived, and he continued paying for the cleanup.

Now, the building had more than adequate incinerators to take care of the trash, but walking down the hall and getting rid of garbage in a responsible manner was clearly too much exercise for Marvin's one hundred or so tenants. They simply opened their windows and tossed the refuse into the courtyard. Marvin repeatedly asked them to stop doing this, but to no avail.

Finally, in frustration, Marvin refused to pay any more fines, and he was hauled into court. A cadre of tenants, screaming that they were Marvin's victims, came to the hearing to vilify him. Why does the garbage continue to pile up, the judge asked? Tongue in cheek, Marvin confessed that each evening he would load up his new car with stinking trash and haul it to Brooklyn to dump in the courtyard he had just paid to clean.

Who are the victims here? Are they the tenants, who apparently do not know how to clean up their own mess? Or is it Marvin, who along with the rest of us play by the rules and pay for other people's mistakes?

As citizens, we have the right to demand responsible behavior from each other, and from our government. If individuals among us live irresponsibly, the rest of us should not be penalized. When it comes to victims, the people screaming loudest are usually the culprits. The *real* victims—the majority of decent people—suffer in silence. This is a peculiarly American sickness.

Don't Blame Me—Blame Everyone Else

How do we solve the problem?

Society must demand that people grow up and accept responsibility. The folks who insist that we continue to tolerate abuse by self-described victims should get the message—not anymore.

In the next pages you will meet lawyers who cannot say no to abusive derelicts, mates who blame the courts because their spouses are not rocket scientists, and people who think the taxpayers owe them a living, not to mention a fully furnished apartment.

The disease of victimization traverses all economic lines, from drug-addicted welfare mothers who keep having babies to clever folks who are forever looking for ways to fleece our social service programs. And a blizzard of buzzwords has been propagated to justify paying homage (and of course money) to irresponsible behavior. Words like prisoners' rights. Criminal rehabilitation. Family preservation. And confidentiality. The words all sound good until you dissect them. So read on.

The decline of personal responsibility is the hallmark of our time, and we cannot simply blame the system for breaking down. With so many people refusing to take charge of their lives, the social service programs designed to be a safety net can no longer handle the load. They are overwhelmed by numbers. These days, *everybody* is a victim.

Courts, judges, legislators, chief executives, social service bureaucrats and community activists all contribute to this breakdown of responsibility. Too often, we are our own worst enemies.

Let me begin with a story that my friend Marvin would understand. One Tuesday morning, David, a veteran legal aid attorney in New York Family Court, came to his office and was surprised to find his door slightly ajar. An unbelievably foul odor came from within as he entered the room.

Inside, the lawyer found a homeless man sleeping on his couch in urine-stained pants. The intruder had obviously spent an active night in the office: He had defecated on a desk filled with files, and had strewn garbage and food waste all over the floor. It was a disgusting, repellent scene.

How did the man get in? Our offices are opposite a small park that separates the criminal courts from the family court building. In recent years, the park has become an outdoor hotel for the homeless, and one of these people somehow broke into the family court building, camping out in David's office.

When I heard this bizarre story, my first question was whether the police had been called. But apparently David would not or could not do that. He felt a strong sense of compassion for the man's economic plight, and simply had him escorted out of the building. That was his "punishment."

The immediate result, of course, was that David's new homeless friend and erstwhile roommate would tell his friends in the park about the wonderful new accommodations he had found. Very warm and inviting, he would tell them, and no one seems to care. Pass it on—the big office down the hall sleeps six!

Who is the victim here? Is it the homeless man who left an obnoxious calling card? Or is it David—and the rest of us—who have been abused? By doing nothing, David reinforced the twisted message we send to victims and victimizers. In our society, the risk of antisocial conduct should be the threat of getting caught. Yet David took that threat away by letting the intruder off the hook. He basically suggested that this conduct was OK.

Common sense—and common decency—dictate another approach. If legal reasoning does not get my point across, a shopping analogy surely will.

Do You Prefer Shoplifting at Macy's or Bloomingdale's?

Macy's and Bloomingdale's in New York are two huge department stores that have serious problems with shoplifting. Assume for a moment that Macy's has a no-arrest policy: If you are caught, they will simply escort you out of the store and tell you not to come back. Meanwhile, Bloomingdale's vigorously enforces the law and arrests people who steal. If you were a would-be shoplifter, which store would you visit—Macy's or Bloomingdale's?

The story of David and his homeless friend is exactly parallel. As supervising judge, I would have instantly had the man arrested. I would have sent a quick, tough message to him and his pals that such conduct was inexcusable: If you are going to act like a pig, do not do it in family court. They might try their luck in criminal court, and hopefully get the same response. Then perhaps on to civil court down the street. If society got tough, maybe some of them would shape up. Or at least defecate in a designated area.

Criminals Are Not Victims, They Are Criminals

In my years on the bench, I have known many lawyers who are strongly committed to representing the poor. Whether they are called legal aid lawyers or public defenders, they share a philosophy that essentially views perpetrators as victims. Even though someone breaks the law, according to their credo, they are victims of much larger social injustices, and must be treated with understanding. This kind of thinking persists even when defenders of the poor and downtrodden themselves become victims, like my friend David.

When we fail to punish aggressors, we all become victims. Maybe the bleeding hearts should wear a sign that says "Mug Me First!" so the rest of us would have a chance. Try that for compassion and understanding.

Lennie Was a Musician, Not a Brain Surgeon

If my court were a classroom, I would call it Responsibility 1-A. Most of the people passing through— lawyers and bureaucrats as well as defendants—would get failing marks. But they would all get straight A's in Victimology.

Take the case of Lennie, a musician. He and his former wife came before me in a dispute over child visitation. They had two children and his ex-wife complained that Lennie had been most irresponsible, failing to honor the visitation schedule they agreed on. She bemoaned his lifestyle and erratic hours, railing that she was a victim in this relationship and that the court system had somehow failed her. Would I put him in jail, she asked?

I was not unsympathetic, but this woman failed to understand that (a) she was not a victim, and (b) the system was not responsible for her problem. She had picked a musician to marry and father her children.

Why should she expect me to wave some wand and turn him into a VIP with banker's hours?

"Madam," I said, "I know you are angered by your husband's itinerant lifestyle and unpredictable hours. But I only have one question for you: Was he a brain surgeon when you met him?" Thankfully, she had a grip on reality and was convulsed with laughter. We resolved the case amicably, and there was no need to put Lennie in jail. I did not change him; that is not my job. She picked him. She had kids with him, and for better or worse—how quickly we forget those words!—this mess was their responsibility. No victims, please.

Don't Just Sit There—Do Something

I sent the same message to Amy and Joe, both in their twenties.

Amy had four children, and Joe had fathered two of them. They were unmarried and quite irresponsible when it came to raising their kids. Indeed, the children had been removed from the home by child welfare authorities because Mom and Dad had left them alone for an hour while "hanging out" in front of their apartment building. It was stupid and selfish behavior, but not the worst case scenario, and when the matter came before me I was anxious to return these children to them. Despite their immature actions, the foster care setting where these kids had been temporarily placed was far worse.

The problem was that Joe and Amy's public housing apartment needed substantial repairs before the children could return. Week after week, I monitored this case to ensure the city was making repairs quickly. Finally, everything was done except for an old refrigerator in the kitchen that had to be removed and some linoleum in the bathroom that had to be replaced.

Suddenly, these two young parents complained that the work was beyond them. It was too much to expect, they whined. Why didn't the city finish the job? They were caught up in red tape and felt victimized. I looked at these folks and shook my head. Joe was six foot one, healthy and strong as a horse. Amy was attractive, and had beautiful hair that probably took four hours to braid. Both seemed intelligent and capable of taking care of themselves.

"Why aren't you back in your apartment right now, resolving these problems?" I asked. "What could possibly be stopping you?" Joe answered that "they gotta move the 'frigerator." For her part, Amy wondered when "they" would get around to finishing her bathroom floor.

I could only take so much of this nonsense, and told them they should be ashamed of themselves. I thought back to the carpet that I removed from the floor of my first apartment, by myself. I thought of the new tile that I laid in my kitchen only last year. Was this work too menial for these folks?

Their four children were being tended to by strangers, and they refused to take the simple steps that would allow them to reunite their family. Who were the victims here? Was it Joe and Amy, waiting for the city to bail them out yet again? Or was it their children—and the rest of us who foot the bill?

We have to stop infantilizing people. We let them get away with outrageous kinds of behavior, because life is "too tough." It is time for all of us to grow up.

If You're a Victim, I'm Dolly Parton

I am weary of hearing about teen mothers and how the deck is stacked against them. Let us face facts: The poor children born into these families are the only real victims. When I encounter a single, unemployed mother on welfare with six or seven children, I do not feel guilty. I feel a sadness for her children, who have little hope of a productive life. One mistake is tolerable, but there is no excuse for six.

The responsibility rests squarely with Mom. We did not conceive these kids; we did not bring them into the world; we did not abuse them. Men and women should not begin families unless they are equipped—mentally and financially—to nurture them. If you flout this rule and have a gaggle of kids, your claim of "victimhood" is bogus. So is your "right" to determine how society will allocate precious resources to support your growing family.

We're Held Hostage to Irresponsibility

I had a stark reminder of this last year, when a visibly pregnant woman came before me and filed a petition to regain custody of her two children. They were in the custody of her maternal grandmother, and apparently doing well. The mother said she had just completed a drug treatment program and was putting her life back together. She was ready to reunite her family.

I asked her some simple questions: "When did you finish the drug program?" "Last month," she replied. "Where do you live?" "In a room with the father of my new baby," the woman answered. "Well," I asked, "if you just came out of a drug rehabilitation program last month, where did you find this new father?" "In the drug program," she said. "You didn't waste any time," I replied.

At this, the smile left her face and she looked insulted. Yet what did she think she deserved, a medal? Here we had two allegedly recovering drug addicts with no job, no home, and no prospects, having a baby. She expected me to give back her two children—mainly because it would entitle her to a larger public housing apartment. She was down and out. Hadn't she suffered enough?

What a sob story! This woman was not a victim, but her children and the public *are* losers. We are held hostage to her irresponsibility. I strongly believe that every drug rehabilitation program should have a tough family planning component, so blessed "accidents" like this do not occur. A woman in one of these programs once complained she did not know what to do with birth control pills. "You're supposed to eat 'em, not smoke 'em!" I replied.

The Cult of Victimhood Is Everywhere

It cuts across race, income and gender. I recently learned of a middle-class New Jersey couple who opened up a local chapter. The husband had been diagnosed with cancer, and before he started chemotherapy—which would make him sterile—he made deposits in a local sperm bank. This way, the couple might still start a family.

Unfortunately, the chemotherapy did not work and he died. A year later, his widow used the sperm to become pregnant. A fine, healthy baby was born. Up to this point, it was a wonderful love story. But then the mother tried to get social security benefits for the child. Her claim was disallowed, because administrators found that the baby had been born two years after her husband's death and was therefore illegitimate. A sympathetic article in the local newspaper profiled this woman, making the government look like a monster.

But who is at fault here? Social security was intended to be a safety net for the children of working people who die unexpectedly and prematurely. This new mother knew exactly what she was doing and, more important, when she did it. Her husband was dead, and *then* she had a child. Yet here she was, asking taxpayers to foot the bill for a new baby. This woman was a lot of things—ambitious, creative and enterprising. But she was no victim.

Neither was Antonio. He told me straightfaced that his welfare benefits were more important to him than the health and safety of his teenage son, George. One day they both came into my court, where George was charged with riding in a stolen car. You may remember him from Chapter 2—he was the young man who had never been in trouble with the law before, yet probation reports said he was not doing well.

His father, a strong-looking man of thirty-two, had been physically abusing his wife for some time. The woman had run away from home at seventeen and married Antonio, and George was born soon thereafter. I learned that the father had been on welfare for thirteen years, while his wife was receiving SSI benefits for chronic asthma. Recently, the boy had stopped attending school. But it was not for the usual reasons. His father had been regularly beating up the mother, and George, now five foot eleven, felt compelled to defend her, especially when Dad got drunk.

The boy had always been a bright student, but now it looked like he was throwing his future away. The probation report recommended that I take him out of this dysfunctional home and put him in an institution somewhere. This was absurd. Why did we have to disrupt George's life, when his father was the main problem in the home? I looked down at this man sternly and told him that, instead of institutionalizing his son, *he* should be the one to move out and leave his troubled family in peace. He became enraged.

"Judge," he protested "welfare wouldn't pay enough for me to live alone!" Why was he being victimized, he asked? Where could he find housing? "Sir," I replied, "I don't care if you move into a refrigerator box and live underneath the highway. You're the problem. You move out!" Once again, we had it backward: George was the victim here, and yet his dad thought we would gladly accommodate a culprit. Not in my country!

Kids like George deserve better. They should be assured a happy childhood, but that is a guarantee their parents must honor. Society cannot monitor every home and correct parental failures. If Mom and Dad fail to measure up, we are all diminished. But it is not our fault, and we should not let misguided guilt distort our policies. If all else fails and society must step in to protect children and itself, I find it irrelevant what abusive parents want or demand.

They had their chance to do the right thing—and they failed. If we must now spend money to repair the damage caused to or by their children, they have *no* right to tell us how to do it. But good luck getting this message across.

Don't Tell Me How to Spend My Money on Your Mistake

Once during hearings on juvenile crime, a group of parents appeared, demanding to speak. No one on the panel knew who they were, but this was a public forum and we were supposed to hear from the people. As it turned out, they were parents of young men who had been convicted of serious felonies and were in state custody. They had gathered to protest that state agencies were not treating them deferentially, and that they were the victims of a sinister, uncaring system. They had not been consulted about the treatment of their children. They rattled off a menu of social services to which they believed their imprisoned sons were entitled.

I sat there and thought to myself: Where do you people get off telling the state how to fix the problems you created? Your children did not become law-abiding citizens, and you bear the responsibility for this. At least be grateful that somebody cares enough to try to rehabilitate these kids.

You're Not Victims of Outrageous Fortune, Folks—You're Just Outrageous

Where did we get the idea that parenthood is sacred, no matter how you raise your kids? If you lack the maturity to raise and nurture a family, your children will suffer. What we need today is a lot less compassion for dysfunctional parents and far more penalties for irresponsible behavior.

Crack use by poor women exploded in the 1980s and we know the devastating results. Hundreds of thousands of children have entered the foster care system because of their addicted mothers, and every year we add more. If we are so worried about victims, let us get results: I once suggested that it should be a crime to give birth to a second crack-addicted baby. You should have heard the feminist groups react! They wanted to remove my heart through my mouth; all they could talk about was poor mothers and their constitutional rights.

I see it differently. Having one baby born with a crack addiction, a low birth weight and other handicaps might be a tragic mistake the first time around. That, however, is where my compassion ends. If the only penalty for having more crack babies is loss of custody, where is the incentive to stop?

If you dare do such a thing twice, we should be able to incarcerate you for a year. The third time, it should be a felony. Women's groups may scream that this victimizes crack mothers, but I am actually quite flexible. When men start giving birth to drug-addicted babies, I will gladly incarcerate them, too.

Ladies, if you want to use drugs, that is your business. If you want to have babies, that is also your business. But if you do both, I will do everything within my power to make your life *very* unpleasant. The legislature must give judges more latitude; there must be tough penalties for intentionally bringing emotionally and physically damaged babies into the world year after year.

This also applies to fathers, who commit their own forms of abuse.

I recently handled the case of a grandmother who was seeking custody of a child who had been in foster care. Everyone agreed that it was in the boy's best interests to live with her, and I was prepared to approve a final order of custody when the child's lawyer said there was a problem with finances.

He told me it would take about six weeks to put the child on Grandma's welfare budget, so what could we do before then? The father, thirty-five, happened to be sitting in court and he looked pretty fit. So I asked why he failed to support his son. He had told me that he had a job and was making decent money in Delaware. Let *him* pay for the boy, I suggested, and give the system a break.

You would have thought I had spouted a string of obscenities. The boy's lawyer began screaming that Grandma had every right to apply for welfare. The child has the right to have a steady source of support, he said, to which I replied, "You bet he does. But not from me and the taxpayers. From his father!"

Who Pays for All This Generosity?

It is amazing how many people are eager to soak the system, especially when it comes to lawyers. In our country, indigent people are given free legal counsel. That is fine and good, but nowhere in the Constitution does it say you are entitled to a free ride. The law need not be an ass and assume that the people who are using legal aid lawyers today will be indigent for life.

Why not charge people for the cost of using a public defender? The debt would be payable to the state when a person gets back on his or her feet. Even if it takes years to pay back, we would create a healthy sense of obligation.

After twenty-five years in the system, I know that many criminal defendants have very little regard for the free lawyers we give them, and even less respect for the judicial system. I deal with smart alecks who regularly miss court dates or show up hours late for hearings with no legitimate excuse. We pay their lawyers regardless, and that should stop. I rarely see people sauntering into court late if they are paying for attorneys out of their own pockets.

Those cases move more smoothly through our judicial system, and it is no wonder. If we want to send a tough message about responsibility, we should require parents to pay for the public lawyers who represent their kids in court.

As a new judge, I had a case involving a young woman who was arrested three times for shoplifting. Her father was an accountant, earning close to six figures a year, yet he refused to hire a lawyer for her. I was compelled to appoint one, at state expense, but not without a warning to dear old Dad: I was going to hold him responsible for the entire amount of the lawyer's bill to the state. I viewed the legal expenses for his sticky-fingered daughter as a necessity, like food, clothing and shelter. When the case was over, he wrote a check for the fee, which came to $700. He still got quite a bargain, because a private lawyer would have charged him three times that amount.

I mailed his check to the program which administers free lawyers. But they returned it, saying this had never happened before and they could not find an account to handle such a deposit! I sent it again—telling them to try harder.

If the Choice Is Your Money or Mine, I Choose Yours

By the way, the same kind of financial requirement should apply when your child breaks the law and is institutionalized. The cost of custody should rest with *you*, not with the state. We should be only secondarily responsible. If you screwed up, folks, why make us victims twice over? What's fair is fair.

It reminds me of the case of a boy from an African

country whose father was employed on a diplomatic mission in New York. The boy went on a robbery spree, targeting six separate victims. His father wisely hired a private attorney, but advised me that he felt more comfortable in court with the services of an interpreter who spoke his native tongue. I secured the interpreter, and when the case was over I presented Dad with a bill for these services, which came to $300. He protested that I was "victimizing" him, but to no avail.

It is an interesting buzzword, "victimizing." Did the father really think I was singling him out for special punishment? Or was it simply a matter of not wanting to pay the money for an extraordinary court proceeding?

His behavior was typical of so many people who use buzzwords to bemoan their fate and avoid personal responsibility. There is no end to them: Victimization. Family preservation. Confidentiality. Sibling reunification. Home builders. Welfare entitlement. Community-based drug programs. They fill up my day and make a mockery of reality-based social reform.

A Blizzard of Buzzwords

In the blizzard of buzzwords, real victims are ignored. If social programs and lofty concepts work, fine. But we should vigilantly weed out the ones that do not. It is time to clean house, and drug programs are a good place to start.

I can say unequivocally that 90 percent of the time, community-based drug programs are ineffective in curing crack addiction. They sound good on paper and have admirable intent, but the hard truth is that while people enter and reenter these units, the only quantifiable result is public money spent. The programs that produce lasting results are long-term, residential efforts that require much greater sacrifice and commitment on the part of an addict.

Why, then, do we keep pouring money into these community programs? The answer is political and economic. There is money to be made in these short-term programs. Somebody is making out like a bandit, and it is certainly not the taxpayer. The only victims here are those people who foot the bill for lousy programs.

There is a simple way to fix this problem: If you are a drug addict whose children have been removed by the state, you must complete a long-term, residential drug treatment program *or* lose custody of your kids. Period. That should be the law—and it would produce instant results. Women shuttle in and out of community-based programs year after year, and sometimes the only thing I can do is hold their children hostage to compliance with a much tougher standard. I tell the mother of a third crack-addicted baby that we will permit the infant and her other children to live with her mother—but *only* if she promises to enter and remain in a residential drug treatment program. Her lawyers may scream that I am violating her rights, and turning her into a victim. My response is, that is her problem.

"Sibling reunification" is another buzzword with a nice ring to it. Ideally, it means that when children are taken from their biological parents because of neglect, the state must try to keep the children together in foster homes. A lovely theory in principle, but not when implemented by the mindless.

Take the case of Joshua, three years old, who had lived with foster parents since birth. His biological mother, a crack addict, had eight children, and the most recent baby was born addicted to cocaine. Joshua's foster parents had been doing a fine job, but did not want any other children in their home. They were not doing it for the money; they seemed to be genuine, caring folks who would give the boy a good, stable life. It was too good to last.

In 1994, Joshua's biological mother had yet *another* baby, and the foster parents were told that unless they took in this new infant to keep the siblings together, the boy would be removed and placed with his maternal aunt, who was caring for his eight brothers and sisters! It was a travesty: Why did Joshua's life have to be distorted because his mother had another baby?

What happens if his maternal aunt suddenly announces that she is tired of all the hassle, and asks the child welfare bureaucracy to find a home that would accept ten children and raise them appropriately? We will have ruined several lives in fealty to a buzzword that, ultimately, satisfies no one.

Hope was another casualty. She was two and a half years old when she was put in a foster home where both parents worked. They had a wonderful teenage son and owned their home. They were educated and committed to Hope's future.

The girl, however, had been the youngest of five children, and her four older siblings—with whom she had never lived—had been placed in the care of their grandmother and an aunt. Neither Grandma or Auntie had ever worked. Neither was educated. After a couple of years, Grandma decided that she now had enough room and could take care of Hope, since one of her sons had just been sentenced to five to fifteen years for armed robbery. His room was now free!

In the name of sibling reunification, the child welfare administration decided it was best to transfer Hope to her grandmother's care. Never mind that a girl was losing perhaps her only chance to live a productive life. Instead of four kids with no future, there would now be five.

I dug in my judicial heels and refused to approve the city's plan. But how many other children risk life and limb through such bureaucratic bungling?

The answer, unfortunately, is "confidential." When it comes to the identities of those who abuse and even murder children, we are more concerned with "confidentiality" than culpability. It may turn out to be the most lethal buzzword of them all, as shown by a recent story in the *New York Times*.

The Ultimate Coverup: Confidentiality

Jesus was three years old when his mother's boyfriend, angered at having water splashed on him, held the toddler underwater in a bathtub until he was unconscious. He arrived in a Bronx hospital emergency room without a pulse or blood pressure, and seemed well on his way to becoming another ugly statistic.

Yet Jesus was lucky: He was dunked in the tub on a day when only cold water poured from the tap, and when he was brought to the hospital, his low body temperature—approximately 77 degrees—had put his vital organs into a state of limbo. Miraculously, doctors were able to raise his temperature gradually, and the boy's heart suddenly began beating again. He survived.

Newspaper accounts identified the boyfriend as well as the boy's mother. Shortly after Jesus was born, he had been brought to an emergency room with a fractured skull, a fractured rib and burns, and officials placed him in foster care, finding his mother responsible for the injuries. She was sentenced to probation. Two years later, however, she regained custody of Jesus after completing a so-called "home rebuilding program," which included parenting classes and counseling.

An obvious question: Who are the geniuses in our child welfare bureaucracy who returned Jesus to his mother and her violent boyfriend? Who is responsible for putting him back in an abusive home? The answers cannot be found in the *New York Times* article, because Human Resources Administration officials routinely refuse to disclose such details for reasons of "confidentiality."

But I ask you: Whose confidentiality is being protected here? Not the boyfriend, because we know his name. Not the mother; she had been cited for neglectful behavior in the past and is in serious trouble again. Not Jesus, whose traumatic experience and photograph were splashed on the front page.

The only people being protected here are caseworkers and other officials, who regularly hide behind a wall of secrecy. God forbid we should know their names. It just might build some accountability into the system, and allow us to identify incompetent bureaucrats whose actions can kill children.

In the last year alone, dozens of babies in New York were murdered or tortured either by their parents or their mothers' boyfriends. In most cases, the abusers were previously reported to authorities by relatives, neighbors and friends, but the records of those incidents are also considered confidential. Again, whom are we protecting here? Who are the victims— and who are the culprits?

If New York statistics are any indication, tens of

thousands of kids in foster care across the country face similar traumas each year. But few people sue governmental officials on behalf of these kids. Most of the time, they are quietly moved to yet another foster home, and the records are again sealed.

In a recent case I handled, a social worker told me that children had been moved to their third foster home. The first placement was in their aunt's home and that lasted only two months; one of the infants had been underfed and was in poor health. The next placement was in a cousin's home. She fed the kids, but eventually gave them back because Mom kept coming by the house demanding money for drugs and screaming, "You're getting all that money for my kids, and some of it's mine." The third placement was in the home of a single mother who had three children of her own. She found the foster kids "too damaged," however, and punished the oldest one by locking her in a closet.

When all these details came to light, the case was hushed up. No charges were ever filed against any of these people. The city simply closed up the foster homes, keeping all of the records confidential. Wouldn't you like to know who investigated these dysfunctional people in the first place? Citizens cannot get decent answers, and even politicians cannot pry loose the details. It is one big bureaucratic secret.

Dozens of cases where kids have been maimed or

murdered never reach public attention, and it is not just because they are poor minority children. It is because of confidentiality rules, which protect inept bureaucrats and a faltering social service system. They do nothing to protect children.

I will never forget the case of two children who had been placed with a foster couple, both caring people. They asked a lot of questions of city officials, however, and demanded services for the children. The city retaliated by moving the children to the home of a single welfare mother with a brood of her own. The original foster couple was devastated. Within six months, the youngest child was beaten to death by one of the foster mom's boyfriends.

It was only then that the Child Welfare Agency, in its wisdom, decided to give back the child who was still alive. No details were disclosed.

Who was protected by this subterfuge? Was it the biological mother, whose abusive behavior caused these children to be placed in foster homes in the first place? Who cares about her! Maybe it was the Child Welfare Agency, which failed to screen adequately the foster home where the youngest child was killed. But who cares about the agency! Consider the foster mother, who permitted this homicide in her home. Do we care about her sensitivities? And what about the boyfriend, who so brutally murdered an innocent? Are his rights to confidentiality important? Get your priorities straight, America.

Forget Buzzwords and Get Back to Reality

What works in one home might fail in another. Children are human beings, not pawns to be shuffled around a game board. I will leave you with a story that shows how flexibility and understanding can sometimes create a happy ending.

Eddie, a bright, precocious boy, had been in a foster home since birth. His mother was a drug addict, in and out of jail, and after four years the state moved to terminate her parental rights. Eddie loved his foster parents, and they adored him. The adoption looked like it would sail through, when all of a sudden the boy's maternal grandfather surfaced, asking for custody of his grandson. He had never laid eyes on him before, and I was naturally skeptical.

But the grandfather was impressive when he first appeared in court. He sounded articulate, seemed intelligent and struck me as someone who was legitimately concerned about his grandson's welfare. He told me candidly that he was a recovering drug addict who had been in a residential treatment program for two years and had been drug-free since his release eighteen months previously. Clearly, he wanted to help his daughter, since he felt partially responsible for her drug addiction. He was a man back on track.

The question was: Should I preserve the biological ties and put Eddie in his grandfather's care or approve the adoption by his foster parents? There are many ways to define a family, and this boy had known no other parents in his entire life. They had nurtured him, and were heartsick at the thought of losing him. Luckily, Grandpa understood.

I terminated the biological mother's parental rights, but told the foster parents about the importance of grandparents. How important it is for a child to have as wide a community of love and affection as possible. When the parties left my courtroom, the foster parents stood in the hall and spoke warmly to the grandfather. He, in turn, treated them with gracious respect.

There were no victims here—only a family that was committed to raising a young boy for years to come. I had a sense they would work it out.

CHAPTER 9

Media Morality: Missing in Action?

Life on the Front Page: A Mixed Blessing

Recently I had a sodomy case scheduled before me for trial. The victim was four years old, and the accused juvenile was fourteen. On the morning of the trial, both sides requested a conference. The prosecutor said he would agree to what we call an adjournment in contemplation of dismissal—which means there would be no conviction. In six months, the juvenile's records would be sealed. The defense was ecstatic.

I said, "If you have no case and if the kid is innocent, the case should be withdrawn." To which the prosecutor replied, "He is not innocent. But the four-year-old is too traumatized to testify, so they can't proceed to trial."

At this point, my instinct for self-preservation kicked in. If I granted the prosecutor's request and the teenager sodomized *another* four-year-old the next month and threw him off a roof, I could just see the headlines: SLAP ON WRIST BY SOFT FAMILY COURT JUDGE RESULTS IN TRAGEDY.

I've spent a quarter of a century building a reputation as a judge who is tough on juvenile crime. In one instant, it would be down the toilet.

The prosecutor was young, but no dummy. He could see the headlines, too, only with *his* name instead of mine. After thirty seconds of deliberation, I rejected this devil's bargain. "Call your first witness," I told him. "I don't have a first witness," he answered. Checkmate. He withdrew the case.

I had not solved the situation to my satisfaction—I couldn't—but I had dodged the potential media bullet. Others are not so lucky. There was once a soft-headed family court judge who, in the late 1970s, paroled a fifteen-year-old on a Friday. It was his third arrest and the second for gun possession. Over the weekend, the kid killed an elderly man during a robbery.

On Monday morning, family court was crawling with news reporters, all demanding an interview with this now-famous judge. But he had barricaded himself in the bathroom of his chambers, foolishly thinking the story would go away if he hid from the press. For his judgment and courage, he got a richly deserved one-way ticket to oblivion when he was not reappointed.

Today, few remember his name.

The Media Should Provide Balance—Not Ballast

I tell these stories to make a point about the communications business and its powerful impact on us. I am always amused by the bickering among our three branches of government as to which is more powerful—the executive, the legislative or the judiciary. Who cares? There is no contest. The media is the single most powerful entity in this country.

Television. Radio. Magazines. Newspapers. They have forced presidential resignation, legislative suicide and judicial impeachment. They determine what we wear, buy and think. They influence whom we love, hate, admire and envy. They decide what we see, hear and feel, where we vacation, dine or seek entertainment. No institution is exempt from their gaze—including our courts.

But power brings responsibility. And these days, a lot of folks are asking disturbing questions about the American media and its social obligations. I believe the media should use its influence realistically to address society's worst plagues. I am convinced that it is an untapped resource.

When it puts its mind to it, the media can be a force for good. It has convinced us to wear seat belts, to not drink and drive. We have absorbed the message about the importance of exercise and low-fat foods. Millions have kicked their nicotine habits because of the steady barrage of media stories.

If the communications business can do all this, why not use the same blunt honesty to portray social misfits as just that, instead of victims who deserve our sympathy? Think of the sweeping changes we might trigger in public policy if the media presented the pariahs in our midst as harbingers of misery, rather than the victims of some amorphous societal neglect. No longer would we feel collective guilt for the misdeeds of a few.

A recent survey of the front pages of major metropolitan newspapers is illustrative.

MARCH 4, 1995: DIFFICULT CUSTODY DECISIONS BEING COMPLICATED BY AIDS

It was Saturday morning and I retrieved the paper from outside my front door. Every day there is a page-one reminder of social problems run amok, and today's fare was a sympathetic piece about mothers with HIV or AIDS. We were told how the system "wrestles" with these mothers' rights to regain custody of kids from foster care versus their children's right to a secure childhood.

The story profiled a woman who "lost" her seven children to foster care. She had left them alone while she went out on a crack binge for several days. This latter fact was barely mentioned. The account traced her three-year quest to regain custody in very positive terms. While she was out "questing," and despite the fact that she was HIV-positive, this lady had two more children and several drug relapses.

This was crucial information, you would think, but readers did not discover it until they were deep into the story. And quite frankly, I am astounded that intelligent people could even *question* whether there is an overriding interest in returning children to such a mother. How selfish and irresponsible must she be before we throw in the towel and finally put the kids' interests first?

There are the kinds of questions I would like to see raised. Does this mother have to maim these children before we cut her off? What about the "nuclear family" of drug addicts and boyfriends these kids will be exposed to when we reunite them in the name of "family preservation"? And who do you think fathered this lady's last two children—some Nobel Prize laureate?

I did not find these questions in the story, and my guess is you would have trouble discovering them in your local newspapers, too. The odds that a convicted mass murderer will be executed are *less* than the odds that this woman's last two babies will die a long and painful death. But where is the editorial clamor for their rights? Where are the candlelight vigils, parades and page-one demands for *their* long-term interests and legal protections?

Let us get it straight: This mother who has been "questing" for custody is not a sympathetic character. She is not a victim. She is a walking lethal injection for her unborn children and unwitting sex partners. And she must be stopped.

Who better to do this than our media? They are responsible for airing these issues—however painful and uncomfortable it may be for some to swallow. It takes courage to jump off the politically correct band-wagon and say that enough is enough. Reporters and editors are always priding themselves on their guts and integrity. Well, let us see the goods.

MAY 5, 1995: ANGUISH IN ERA OF AIDS, CHOOSING TO HAVE BABIES

Even the headline sounds bizarre, but when it comes to the media, nothing surprises me. Why would any-one with AIDS or HIV choose to have a baby? How could they possibly put their own selfish desires ahead of a vulnerable, innocent child who might be doomed to suffer a short and painful life?

This news story chronicled two women, one of

whom had seven children and was on welfare. One baby had already died at twenty-two months, but here she was "wrestling" with the question of whether she should have yet another child.

The key question this news story should have asked—and did not—is about the children's rights. Whether this woman died or her children died, the kids would suffer. She had singlehandedly created a world of misery for them, and she was *not* a sympathetic figure. Yet that is not how this news story read.

I am not blindly criticizing the media. Sometimes, they tell stories with a sense of public outrage that serves us well. I only wish they would do it more often. It would be a blessing if they chose their topics—and their targets—more carefully, so their full power to do good would be unleashed.

Teen pregnancy would be a great place to start.

The Message? Teen Pregnancy Is Stupid

The estimated annual cost to the public for the more than one million teenage pregnancies this year will be $34 billion. All our studies, blue ribbon panels and "special needs" programs have failed to reverse this trend, and I am proposing an entirely new approach: A full-blown, take-no-prisoners public information campaign that would saturate every household with the message that teenage pregnancy is not simply immoral, wasteful or unhealthy—it is stupid.

Teenagers would get this message very quickly. A fiscal nightmare? They couldn't care less. Bad for the nation's long-term moral health? Gag me with a spoon. But stupid, they understand. We should tell them that a girl who gets pregnant is dumb. Decidedly uncool. A fool, a jerk. Imagine a media campaign with teen celebrities telling their peers in sarcastic TV ads that dropping out of school and becoming a mom at fifteen or sixteen is for morons. Period.

Here is where Madison Avenue advertising firms and TV, radio and newspaper folks could make a huge contribution. We should say *no* to teenage parenting in a way that rattles our young Romeos and Juliets. Forget the warnings about AIDS and VD. They have not worked. Tell a teenager she is a fool and maybe she will listen.

Bring Back the B-Word—or Pay the Consequences

These days, nobody likes to talk about the B-word—birth control—but it is time we face facts. Teenagers who are stupid enough to engage in sex should use it. End of discussion. I am tired of constitutional debates and public forums that turn into pointless shouting matches. Our editorial pages should get the message across once and for all: Without the B-word, we *all* pay.

No matter what we do, kids probably will not stop

having sex. But at least we will get it through their heads that for children to have children is stupid. I am tired of all the weepy portraits, the yawn-inducing profiles of teenage moms and their oh-so-difficult lives. Cut through the baloney and tell the truth.

Some people say that a public health crisis caused this problem. Others blame our schools. A good many say it is caused by peer group pressure. Well, we could point our fingers forever, or we could go right to the source—to Jack and Jill in the backseat of the family car—and level with them bigtime:

Don't be suckers, but if you insist, use birth control.

Maybe we could also appeal to their sense of family pride. If you read deeply enough into newspaper stories about juvenile delinquency, you will invariably find that the mothers of criminals were teenagers when their kids were born. The pattern is obvious, and we should have the courage to point it out: Your chances of having a kid who turns into a hoodlum increase dramatically if you are a teenage parent. Is this what you want to bring into the world? Wise up.

FEBRUARY **17, 1995:** AN INTIMATE LOOK AT WELFARE: WOMEN WHO'VE BEEN THERE

If you read this newspaper piece, as I did, you got a sympathetic look at a couple of women who managed to extricate themselves after years of welfare dependency. The stories were hopeful and generally upbeat. But none of them portrayed the kind of women I see in my courtroom everyday, who are second- and third-generation welfare recipients. There was no mention of the outright criminal behavior and financial deceit that so often colors life on the dole.

Worse, there was an unspoken assumption in the story that taxpayers have no right to ask questions about these women's decision to have more children. The writer seemed to have little patience with the idea that our government might cap the benefits paid to such recipients. "I have a problem with the government getting into bed with me," said an angry welfare mother. "I don't think white men should sit up in a room and make a law to degrade women."

Well, lady, let me tell you about *my* problem. I have a problem with welfare recipients like you who think the community owes them decades of support. I have a problem with parents who disregard a baby's right to a secure childhood and a hopeful future by having children they cannot afford. But most of all I have a problem with community rabble-rousers—and knee-jerk supporters—who vilify anyone who dares to question our support of the chronically irresponsible.

Get real, folks. If someone has their hands in your pockets, it is very much your business. And if the media does not think so, it is part of the problem rather than the solution.

Alternatives to Prison:
Whose Rights Come First?

I am always amused by the sympathetic articles and TV stories about so-called "alternatives to incarceration" programs. The way they're portrayed, one would think these criminals were a varsity team and the program directors philanthropists. The problem is, reporters do not always do their homework, and therefore we only get half the story. They leave out the majority of criminals who, despite these alternative programs, become repeat offenders.

We have our priorities backward—and it affects our prisons as well. The same folks pushing for jail alternatives are selling the idea that if we *must* put criminals behind bars, we owe them a full menu of rehabilitation programs.

God forbid these hoodlums should simply serve out their sentence and then obey the law when they get out. How insensitive! say their advocates. How uncaring and uncharitable! The media has played along, echoing the idea that we need to *do* things for these people—that we owe them special care.

My friends, we do not owe them a damn thing.

They broke the peace. *They* ruined someone's life. All we owe them is jail. The process of putting them where they belong and keeping them there is expensive enough. Who cares if prison is a miserable existence? Hopefully, if we make it so unpalatable, criminals will think twice about returning.

As for the media, it should do a better job of clarifying responsibility. If society decides to pay for costly rehabilitation programs, it is only because society is trying to protect its long-term interests. These programs are society's insurance, not a prisoner's right.

If Sirhan Sirhan or Charles Manson never achieves inner peace—or a Ph.D.—I would not lose a moment's sleep.

MARCH **20, 1995:** CITY TO CUT FOSTER CARE GRANTS FOR CHILDREN

It sounded so heartless. New York, pressed to cut billions from its deficit, would no longer give foster children $500 apiece as a so-called "discharge grant" when they were returned to their parents. The article quoted angry child welfare advocates, who bitterly protested the city's "insensitivity."

But it only told half the story. Here is the other half—just for balance. Let us say that four children have been in kinship foster care with their grandmother for four years. When they were first placed with Grandma, the city provided each of the kids with their own bed, dresser, clothing and other essentials. Every month, Grandma received $500 to $1,000 in payments for each child, in addition to her existing public assistance checks. Not a bad deal.

Now, it is time for Mom to get out of drug rehab and become a full-time caretaker. What she wants— and what the city is no longer prepared to give her—is another $500 apiece for each kid to buy new furniture and clothes.

"A vital service is gone," complains one advocate. "It's an outrage." Well, where are the *old* beds and dressers? Did they all go to furniture heaven? I have worked all my adult life and never replaced my kids' furniture every three or four years. We managed to get by just fine with the old stuff. Starting new is nice, but not with somebody else's money.

I wish the media could have conveyed that message or at least provided the reader with all the facts. Every day the front pages of our newspapers and the lead stories on TV and radio are filled with stories that cry out for some kind of moral perspective—or at least a sense of balance.

Crack Babies: Coming to a Movie Screen Near You

In the mid-1980s, when the crack epidemic exploded, I wanted to shock some sense into the mothers of addicted babies who were streaming through my court.

I had an idea: As these women sat outside, waiting for their hearings, we would show them a short film of the birth of a premature, drug-addicted baby suffering the tremors of withdrawal. It would be an ugly, unforgettable sight, and we would run the video every day, from nine-thirty A.M. until the court closed at five P.M. Hopefully, these mothers would get a jolt of reality.

"Too harsh!" whined some critics. "A cold thing to do!" barked others. But too harsh and too cold for whom? Surely not for these babies, who are wracked with pain the minute they draw breath. Surely not for the society that must pay for this billion-dollar tragedy. Would it embarrass the mothers who had caused these dreadful human problems? Maybe that is just what they need.

Again, this is an area where the media could be of help. Some public-minded outfit—a network or film company, perhaps—could produce such a film with a good, punchy narration. I cannot imagine it would cost them that much money, and the social good they might generate would make it all worthwhile.

This is not the kind of show that would boost your Nielson ratings, yet any executive who cared enough to do it might get an even greater reward. People may not listen to experts when they are lectured about the crime and disgrace of crack babies. But they sure do believe what they see on television.

I could not overcome the politically correct, liberal left who blocked my crack film proposal. That should not stop us from trying again.

Costly Trials: Make the Media Pay

You are glued to your TV set, watching the O.J. trial. Pass the popcorn, but ask yourself the question: Is this a public service or media spectacle? I think it is entertainment, and Americans who pay for these multimillion-dollar trials should recoup part of the bill from the people who are raking in millions.

These trials are regularly interrupted by four minutes of commercials, touting everything from breakfast cereals to feminine hygiene. Such ads generate big bucks for the networks, who do not pay a dime for the actors, sets, film and other costs. It is cream money for them, twenty-four hours a day. They are not paying for the main course, and they are not paying for the dessert.

With all this cash rolling in, you would think our TV friends might share the wealth when it comes to public spectacles that cost them nothing. While television networks are getting rich off O.J. and the Menendez brothers, *you* are picking up the tab. Since all the media has to do is show up with a television camera, it should shoulder some of the financial burden when trials go beyond news and become entertainment.

You do not get Tom Hanks to shoot a movie out of the goodness of his heart, and our courtrooms are not free, either. We should demand that a portion of the media profits from these public circuses help pay back the costs.

Wardens Versus Addicts:
Who Are the Heroes?

Sometimes, the media creates a bizarre pantheon of heroes. I have never read a story about a prison warden who runs an efficient jail getting a humanitarian award. Nor have I heard of a tough, no-nonsense judge being honored by the community.

I have, however, seen a TV profile about a woman in the South Bronx who has devoted her life to rescuing drug addicts from infection by giving them free needles in exchange for their old ones. She believes that America has become callous to their plight. She says she is discouraged and ashamed of the citizens' inhumane response to "afflicted addicts."

Well, forgive me for not dabbing my eyes. In the TV show about her, I watched addicts dump a weekly supply of syringes on her table, fifty or more apiece. What the hell did she think they put in those needles—soda pop?

They were all shooting heroin, which is deadly and very expensive. Since none of these characters looked like they worked on Wall Street or anywhere else, I knew that the money to support their $300-a-day habits came from victims: people who were killed, maimed or, if they were lucky, only emotionally traumatized for life. Where was the recognition of *these* victims in the television piece? Where was the moral perspective about *them*?

I have no patience with social programs that keep junkies hooked and fuel a dangerous cycle of crime and addiction. Maybe the glowing media profiles of "heroin heroines" could focus instead on the long-term, residential drug treatment programs that actually seem to work on occasion. They are the only programs I am willing to subsidize, because they give addicts a choice—even if it is as simple as killing themselves instead of an innocent stranger.

I'm Robbing You Because Dad Left Home

Drug crime is never pretty. Recently, a local newspaper told of two drug-addicted women who went on a violent robbery spree. Most of their fifteen victims were elderly, and they were either beaten or pistol-whipped.

"Maybe we should have given them free needles," said one community organizer, trying to "empathize" with these women. What a waste of time. One of these criminals was the daughter of a minister. She was a high school dropout with five out-of-wedlock children. All were living in kinship foster care with Grandma. The story went on to say that "in many such cases, [these] suspects are single mothers pushed to the other side of the law to support their children, because the kids were abandoned by their fathers."

But what did that have to do with these women? There were no kids to care for in either case. The

public was supporting them. These were two preda-
tors, who tormented senior citizens. They were totally
lacking in humanity, period, end of story!

MAY **12, 1995:** BUDGET CUTS TO HURT PREVENTIVE SERVICES FOR FAMILIES

I will leave you with one last page-one story. Here, the
article warned that impending budget cuts would dev-
astate counseling programs for families in need. It
began sympathetically: "Denise Richardson was 18,
pregnant with her second daughter, when her
boyfriend was murdered."

Whatever other social services were driveled over
in this piece, there was not a single word about the
one "program" that Denise needed more than any
other to bring some sense back into her troubled
young life: birth control.

America is falling apart and we do not have time
for pretend solutions. If we are going to talk about our
many social problems—and that is one of the media's
chief obligations—we have to talk honestly, openly
and fearlessly, on page one and in prime time. We
need candor in communications and courage in pre-
sentation as never before. The media could be the
instrument of rejuvenating American morality.

CHAPTER 10

Stoking My Fire

I am often asked, How can you stay in your job for so many years with its daily human misery? The answer is that occasional success stories make it worthwhile and rejuvenate me. Here are a few stories from a court that rarely creates human happiness. None of them has a classic storybook ending, because there are never perfect solutions in family court.

The complexity of human problems rarely fits neatly into the four corners of rules. People are asymmetrical; laws are always a perfect square. As a judge, your purpose is to find a just and logical solution—to leave a family in better condition than it was when it came to you. Sometimes you must be creative. This is not judicial activism, it is common sense.

The payoffs can be extraordinary, as you will see

from the stories of John, Michelle, Julie and the boy from Zimbabwe. But in each case, judges have to walk that extra mile, take time to ferret out the facts and reject platitudes and pleasant-sounding buzzword solutions.

Decisions based on garbage, masquerading as information, can produce malodorous results. Digging for facts is often dangerous, because comfortably ensconced bureaucrats don't like people asking embarrassing questions. But rattling their cage can be rewarding when it makes a difference.

His Name Was John

John had set fire to a mattress in the elevator of his apartment house and was charged with arson. Fortunately, no one was hurt, yet it could have been a tragedy. He appeared before me in court with his mother for arraignment on the charges. A routine case—or was it?

John was a short, plump boy with a glazed-over look and a distinct twitch. His mother was disheveled and slow to respond to questions. He was her only child. She sat very close to him, practically leaning on him with her hands clasped over his. The probation department told me that he had not been in school regularly for two years—that he was in a special class for emotionally disturbed children and had been on medication for years.

I had substantial misgivings about this mother's ability to supervise him, and held him in juvenile detention for two weeks. When he returned to court, he appeared slightly agitated, but his eyes were remarkably clear. His lawyer demanded at his mother's insistence that I order Juvenile Corrections to give him his medications. I asked John whether he had been given his medicine and he replied, "no." I asked him how he felt, and he answered that he felt OK, but "funny."

Before I ordered him to be medicated, I directed a complete physical and psychiatric examination. The report I received was astounding and heartbreaking. This thirteen-year-old boy had been on medication since he was three, not because of his need, but because his mother—who was marginally retarded— was having difficulty handling a normal, active three-year-old.

Some quack doctor at a clinic decided that the best prescription would be to medicate the boy so that his deficient mother could handle him. John spent the next ten years in a fog.

Now he was thirteen, functionally illiterate, and had become the companion to his mother, who depended on him for everything. When he was not with her, her drinking—which had been under control—now consumed her.

There was little question that unless I removed him from his home, he would be forever lost. He might be anyway, but he should at least have a chance. He was resistant and his mother hysterical at the thought of his being away. John spent three years away from home. At first, he was miserable. But within a few months I began to receive letters from him. The quality of these letters improved steadily. He began to read, write and communicate with a clear head.

When I last saw him he was sixteen, tall, thin and bright-eyed, and he no longer twitched. He told me he was ready to go home. He was strong enough and his mother needed him. He was indeed ready.

Her Name Was Michelle

Michelle had three children. She had been abusing drugs for three years. When her third child was born drug-addicted, the city began neglect proceedings against her. I removed the children, placed them in foster care and made it clear that she was to be drug-free for at least a year before I would return her kids.

Michelle was smart and one of the few drug program success stories. She had been drug-free for eighteen months and was ready to reclaim her children. I was ecstatic, but there was a glitch. Michelle did not have an apartment. Three caseworkers and one supervisor assigned to her case were useless. No one was ready to break a sweat to unify this family. Michelle's two older children missed their mother and were miserable with strangers in foster care. Meanwhile, the baby had naturally become attached to her foster mother and I knew the transition for this toddler would become more difficult with every month we wasted.

Eventually, Michelle found an apartment. But the caseworker lost the paperwork necessary for the landlord. She found a second apartment. It was lost after a supervisor, who finally found the paperwork, put it at the bottom of her "things to do" pile. It was not an emergency to this overworked bureaucrat.

The mother's strength in overcoming addiction was being tested by an inept bureaucracy. She was doing her best and needed a boost.

Then some little bird must have called a reporter from the *New York Times*, who profiled her story. Within forty-eight hours of this embarrassing article, the bureaucrats became energized, found the paperwork and helped her secure the apartment.

Between the city, her lawyer and my basement, Michelle's apartment was furnished and the children returned. Hopefully a happy ending. The media embarrassed the city into doing its job.

Her Name Was Julie

Julie came from a middle-class family and was raised in New Jersey. She was seventeen when she left home, came to New York and hit the streets strung out on drugs.

At eighteen, she delivered a premature baby girl in a New York hospital. A neonatal nurse, while changing the bedding in her incubator, placed her under warming lights. But the nurse was distracted and forgot about the little baby, who was severely burned on both legs by the lights.

The city filed a neglect case against Julie three months later, when the baby was to be discharged from the hospital. They demanded that I place the child in foster care in New York. But why not release the baby to her grandparents, I asked, especially since they had maintained a vigil at her hospital bed for three months? The city attorney argued that I could not release the child until an interstate investigation of the grandparents' home in New Jersey was completed. I knew from experience that this investigation would take six months to a year.

The paperwork process goes something like this: The forms must be processed in the city and then sent to Albany. Then Albany sends them to New Jersey, and they are transmitted to the town in New Jersey where the grandparents reside. A caseworker from New Jersey would ultimately get around to making a home visit, preparing a report and transmitting the report to Albany, which would notify New York City if the home was satisfactory. Just think of all the bureaucrats handling these details.

Now, these grandparents lived a half hour from New York City. I suggested that one of the three or four social workers assigned to this case might be dispatched immediately to do the home inspection. "Oh, *no!*" It is not permitted by their union contract. They cannot be sent out of state. I could send them four hundred miles to the Canadian border, but I could not send them to Teaneck. I adjourned the case to the following Friday in the afternoon and directed that the baby be produced in court.

One of the caseworkers was a real star and, without approval from her supervisors, made the trek to New Jersey on her own time. Her report: The home was great. The city attorney was nonplused by the report and insisted that without a formal interstate investigation the child could not be released.

Well, it was Friday at four P.M. during the summer and the chances of finding an appeals judge to stay my order were slim to none. So I called the court nursery where the baby had been brought by the caseworker, and ordered that she be released to her grandparents.

Two weeks later, the baby's mother appeared in court. It was the first time I had seen Julie. She was a pale, thin kid with dirty clothes and oily blond hair. She was accompanied by some rock creature who wanted to be declared the baby's father. Clearly, he smelled the color of money from a lawsuit against the hospital. These two druggies were in agreement in insisting that I declare him to be the child's father.

Usually, if the parties agree, the court complies. But I had misgivings in this case, since this man would demand custody if he was recognized as the father. Considering the way he looked, I wouldn't give him custody of a cocker spaniel. I adjourned the case for three months and ordered blood tests. As they were leaving the courtroom, someone—I cannot imagine who—might have suggested to this man that the blood for such a test is drawn with an eight-inch needle from the eye!

Anyway, I never saw him again and hopefully he will never touch any part of the $4.5 million the child was awarded to settle her lawsuit against the hospital. I get a picture and a letter every Christmas from the grandparents. The baby is beautiful and doing fine.

The Boy Was from Zimbabwe

He was eight years old, and lived with his two sisters, mother and diplomat father in Queens, New York. When his teacher noticed a pattern of black and blue marks and large bumps on his head, she sent him to the school nurse, who found the boy's body covered with belt marks. The sobbing child broke down and told officials that he was regularly beaten by his father in the basement of his home. Child Welfare responded, putting the boy in foster care and filing an abuse case against both parents.

At the first hearing, representatives from the U.S. State Department accompanied by the parents and their lawyer argued that the state court had no jurisdiction to hold the boy. His father was a diplomat from Zimbabwe, they said, and was protected by immunity. The judge—over strenuous objections by the boy's lawyer, and after careful research—dismissed the case and directed that the boy be returned to his father from foster care.

The embarrassment and humiliation of the parents was surely to be visited on this child. At the time of this case, I was the supervising judge in Manhattan. Other than some scanty newspaper articles I had read about this boy, I knew nothing about the case. On Saturday morning, the phone rang in my home. It was the attorney who represented the boy, and she had a most unorthodox request. Would I hear her petition to delay the return of the boy based on some alleged "newly discovered" facts?

I asked under what theory she was approaching a Manhattan judge, since the case had originated in the borough of Queens. Her response was flimsy. Clearly they were looking for time to prepare their client and, perhaps, put a mechanism in place to at least monitor the father. I was in a bind. The Queens judge was right on the law. But they were counting on the maverick in me not to turn them down, and they were right.

I told them that if they could gather all the attorneys and the State Department people at my home on Sunday, I would listen to their request. The next day, a cadre of lawyers arrived. The State Department attorney was outraged that I would even contemplate such an order. He told me that it could cause a diplomatic incident with a friendly country, Zimbabwe, with far-reaching repercussions. I answered that before they arrived, I had gone through every closet and cupboard in my home. It was, in my opinion, typical of most American homes, and I could not find one blessed thing that was made in Zimbabwe! Therefore, I reasoned, who the hell cares if Zimbabwe gets in a snit? I signed the order.

It took several months of legal wrangling in the state and federal courts before the boy was returned to his parents. A plan to have the Red Cross monitor his safety was put in place. It was not a perfect ending—but it was better.

Conclusion

People, Not Government, Create Opportunity

If I had to boil this book down to one final phrase, it would be that people, not government, create opportunity. America's families are in trouble. The prescription has been to give them more social programs, and that philosophy has failed. Self-discipline, individual accountability and responsible conduct is the answer. It has always been the answer, but America got lost. It is time to get back on course.

Simple human nature tells us that things earned and paid for with your own money are cherished and cared for. Take education: When a child goes to college and Pop is picking up all the bills, missing class is no big deal. It is a four-year party with a diploma at the end, if you are lucky. Nowadays, kids are stretching four years into six. But just watch the difference in attitude when that same kid has to work to pay his or her tuition. They hit the books big-time.

Did you ever notice how kids who are slobs at home all of a sudden become Mr. Clean when they rent their own pads? I never knew my children could pick up— let alone fold—their own clothes until they got their own apartments. The metamorphosis occurred the first time they signed a rent check.

Remember the first car you bought for your child? You were as excited as they were, but if your experience was anything like mine, they were far more responsible toward the first car they bought with their own money. Now how, you may ask, does that relate to the crisis in American society today?

I have seen so many programs that are society's giveaways: housing, welfare, special education, free medical care, free transportation, adoption subsidies, social security disability for alcoholics and drug addicts. The list is endless, and the results have not produced a more responsible or productive population. There may be a few isolated success stories paraded by the media, but the whole picture does not justify the billions spent by taxpayers.

Add to these direct costs the price tag for bureaucracies that exist to administer these programs—and you can identify even more billions spent by government to "provide" opportunity. The track record is shoddy.

Joann was addicted to crack. She was twenty-three, pretty and bright, and came from a lovely family. Her mother was a bank teller, and had cared for Joann's three-year-old son for two years. Kinship foster care, of course. After a twenty-four-month residential drug program, Joann came to court ready to resume the care of her child. The city attorney argued that before the boy could be returned, Joann had to open up a public assistance case and get a subsidy from the city for an apartment. Joann readily agreed, but I almost had a stroke.

"Welfare?" I shouted. "Oh, no! She is going to get a job."

Well, you would have thought that I just maligned the Pope. "No welfare," I said, "that's hopeless. You have come too far to get on the welfare spiral." Then I adjourned the case for eight weeks for Joann's job search.

When Joann returned to court two months later, she had been employed full-time for six weeks at a Roy Rogers restaurant. She looked terrific, and although she was not crazy about the job, it was a beginning. Joann needed a nudge.

In deciding these cases, responsible behavior should be the benchmark and deviation discouraged. Emma's story is proof of that. For many years, a wonderful elderly lady worked as a cleaning person in family court. Emma never missed a day's work, and as I arrive early, we would chat every morning. Several years ago, I learned that her daughter, a former drug abuser, was dying.

Emma had assumed the responsibility of caring for her three grandchildren. I asked whether she was getting any financial help for them, but she replied that the grandkids were *her* responsibility, that they were her family. She would take care of them for as long as she was able to get up and go to work.

That same day, another grandmother—this one getting $2,500 a month from the state for her grandchildren—told me in court that if the city cut off her money, they could take the kids, too.

Emma retired last year, caring for her grandchildren by herself for as long as she was physically able. She believed it was her responsibility, and she was right.

If Emma now needed our community's help, she should get it. But if our resources are depleted by those who shirk their responsibility, the Emmas of the world will go without help when they need it. This is simply unfair.

Educating our nation's children is the only way to ensure our future as a great country. A free public education is the right of every child and the vast majority of students yearn to educate themselves and become productive adults. But the right to education must be equated with responsibility. If you abuse that right by your behavior, you lose it. Unfortunately, the behavior of a few can turn the hopes of many into pipe dreams. In many schools, more time is spent maintaining order than teaching. Disruptive behavior in school—carrying guns or knives—must result in swift, immediate expulsion.

We diminish all of our children by paying homage to some esoteric sense of fairness, and catering to the few who break the peace. If they cannot behave, they should be out.

As a citizen, you enjoy the right to use the judicial system. But you do not have the right to abuse the judicial system. Richard Loritz, awaiting trial for shooting his ex-girlfriend six times, recently filed suit against his jailers for refusing to provide him with dental floss. He complained in his $2,000 lawsuit that he suffered four cavities as a result. This abuse of our courts is unacceptable and wasteful, and must be discouraged.

In all these matters, our question should not be "Who are the needy?" but rather "Why are they needy?" If a person's life is chaotic because of circumstances beyond their control—like birth defects, fire, flood or earthquakes—Americans will traditionally rally to their support. But if someone's social condition is caused by their own irresponsibility, they are in no position to demand that we assume their self-inflicted burdens.

I started this book with my father's words, and will

end it with some of his best advice. He told me to live my life by a simple word: KISS. Keep It Simple, Stupid. It was good advice, and might be another national anthem:

> If you want to eat, you have to work.
>
> If you have children, be prepared to take care of them.
>
> If you break the law, it is your fault. Be prepared to pay.
>
> If you tap the public purse, be prepared to account.

The Constitution guarantees every citizen the right to pursue opportunity. It does not require the government to provide that opportunity. Beyond creating an atmosphere—legal and social—that enables people to grow, no one is owed anything.

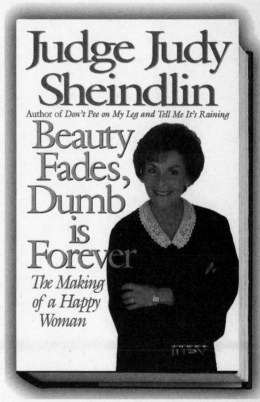